the arts, popular culture, and social change

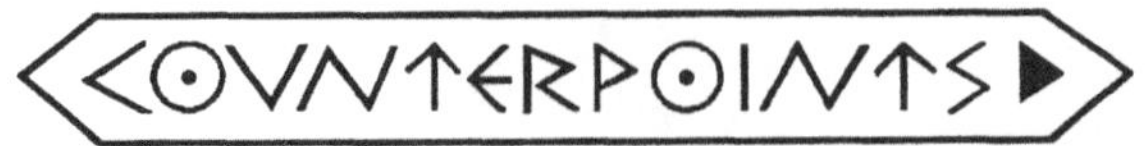

Studies in the Postmodern Theory of Education

Joe L. Kincheloe and Shirley R. Steinberg
General Editors

Vol. 142

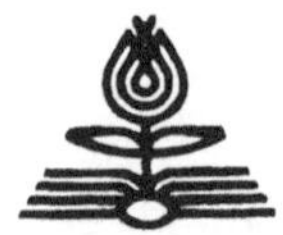

PETER LANG
New York • Washington, D.C./Baltimore • Boston • Bern
Frankfurt am Main • Berlin • Brussels • Vienna • Oxford

Landon E. Beyer

the arts, popular culture, and social change

PETER LANG
New York • Washington, D.C./Baltimore • Boston • Bern
Frankfurt am Main • Berlin • Brussels • Vienna • Oxford

Library of Congress Cataloging-in-Publication Data

Beyer, Landon E.
The arts, popular culture, and social change / Landon E. Beyer.
p. cm. — (Counterpoints; vol. 142)
Includes bibliographical references and index.
1. Arts and society—United States. 2. Popular culture—United States. 3. Aesthetics. 4. Arts—Study and teaching—United States. 5. Popular culture—United States.
I. Title. II. Counterpoints (New York, N.Y.); vol. 142.
NX180.S6 B49 700'.1—dc21 99-052523
ISBN 978-0-8204-4943-2
ISSN 1058-1634

Bibliographic information published by **Die Deutsche Nationalbibliothek**.
Die Deutsche Nationalbibliothek lists this publication in the "Deutsche Nationalbibliografie"; detailed bibliographic data are available on the Internet at http://dnb.d-nb.de/.

Cover design by Nona Reuter

The paper in this book meets the guidelines for permanence and durability of the Committee on Production Guidelines for Book Longevity of the Council of Library Resources.

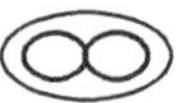

29 Broadway, 18th floor, New York, NY 10006
www.peterlang.com

Printed in the United States of America

To Linda, with gratitude for your support and encouragement

Contents

Introduction		ix
Chapter 1	Modern Theories of Aesthetic Experience	1
Chapter 2	The Meaning and Significance of Art	25
Chapter 3	Education and Cultural Reproduction	47
Chapter 4	The Arts and Social Possibility	67
Chapter 5	Art, Schooling, and Social Action: Toward New Possibilities	89
Chapter 6	Aesthetic Experience for Teacher Preparation and Social Change	109
Chapter 7	The Arts as Personal and Social Communication: Popular/Ethical Culture in Schools	129
Epilogue:	Creating New Worlds	147
Index		155

Introduction

Some recent theoretical analyses and artistic phenomena have fundamentally altered the ways we have understood the arts and aesthetic experience. These challenges to traditional understandings of the aesthetic also suggest possibilities for the transformation of art and aesthetic education in the schools, and possibilities for thinking about teaching as an art form. The present volume consists of a series of integrated chapters which, in analyzing and furthering these changes in how we approach and value the arts, also consider the possibilities for recreating educational practices.

As various chapters in this book will demonstrate, more critical literatures on the nature of education and schooling have also been developed in the last couple of decades. A number of scholars and classroom teachers have thought carefully and deeply about the possible ways in which we might redefine the purposes of education and the social and moral roles of educational practice. This is not to suggest that previous eras have not seen efforts to critically reconstruct school practice. It is, rather, a call to continue to consider ways in which the theoretical analyses and criticisms that have been made of educational institutions and their social contexts may lead to specific classroom practices that construct emancipatory forms of education.

Throughout the history of the creation and appreciation of the arts, as well as through the traditions in aesthetic theory, there have developed schools of thought that have been more or less dominant: the search for the "essence" of the art object in Platonic thought, the fascination with beauty as the central component of works of art, and a commitment to significant form as the defining feature of the arts. While no one approach to the arts or aesthetic theory has been able to maintain its dominance over the long haul, there have been significant periods of time within particular societies and groups in which people's understanding of the value and place of art has been shaped by artistic and aesthetic traditions.

Moreover, as we have become more aware in the recent past—and as this book demonstrates—in order to understand the meaning and value of the arts, we must situate them within the cultural, social, political, economic, and ideological contexts out of which they emerge and from which a significant part of their meaning is derived. This perspective places the arts within a complex, often contradictory set of tendencies and valuations, making the understanding of any particular work of art much more complicated than its meaning when filtered through, say, theories that hold significant form or beauty as the central foci for artistic appreciation.

The chapters in this book are aimed at clarifying the dominant traditions of modern aesthetic theory and showing how they have affected the role, purpose, and value of the arts. They also explore, through a variety of theoretical lenses, the ways in which the relation of the arts to other structures and phenomena can be understood. Collectively, these chapters provide an indication of the divergence that is possible within the domain of the arts and the appreciation of particular forms of art.

Chapters 4 through 7 explore more concretely the possibilities of reconstructing educational policies and practices that reflect (and in turn further) a contextualized theoretical perspective. This applies not only to the domain of art education specifically, but to the more general possibilities for an aesthetic education and for the role of popular culture in society and in the public schools.

Behind the philosophical ideas and issues that are centrally important to this volume stands an essentially moral commitment to changing the current role of the arts in mainstream U.S. society and altering the realities of schooling. The tendencies of many schools to create students who are intellectually apathetic, who value linear thinking, who refrain from questioning those in authority, who engage in isolated and individualizing work, and who acquire ideologically impregnated views of what it means to be "human," for example, have been well documented. This is not to suggest that schools uniformly do this, or that teachers have intentionally or consciously sought such outcomes. On the contrary, the work of many dedicated, hardworking teachers has provided evidence of the possibilities of education reversing the tendencies toward intellectual apathy and linear thinking. This is made more problematic because of some of the deeply embedded educational and ideological phenomena in American society generally, as they promote forms of cultural reproduction that serve dominant interests. The structure of schooling—whose knowledge gets taught there, what kinds of evaluative practices and social relations are promoted, the traditions on which we have relied in thinking about curriculum and pedagogy—has often served to promote perspectives and values that replicate larger cultural and social phenomena.

This book seeks to develop a framework for understanding and enhancing the value of the arts. It attempts to add another dimension to the process of developing more progressive alternatives in public education, as we formulate alternative visions and practices in the arts that can alter the current realities of school life and the personal, social, and cultural realities with which they are connected.

Chapter 1

Modern Theories of Aesthetic Experience

As we consider the nature of aesthetic experience, it is useful to stipulate a commonly made distinction between "the arts" and "aesthetic experience." We can understand "art" to refer to any humanly constructed object or event that focuses on the perceptible qualities of that object or event; in short, an art object must be "artifactual," or constructed by someone. This is true even when the artifact may not have been consciously crafted by that person to be a work of art. When we experience and interact with certain artifacts, we find ourselves engaged in sustained attention to the qualities of that object, and we try to understand what the object represents. Appropriate ways to discern and make sense of particular forms of art are often a matter of some debate, as people focus on different elements of the work or bring to bear distinct preferences or points of reference. "Aesthetic experiences," on the other hand, are generated by our attention to art objects that are humanly constructed as well as those natural phenomena and events for which there is no artist who created the phenomena to which we attend. The play of colors and the contrasts of shadow and light in a landscape at a particular hour of the day, the rhythm and patterns of a meandering mountain stream, and so on, provide occasions for paying attention to the play of colors, sounds, and contrasts whose qualities are often quite engaging.

Questions regarding the nature of art and aesthetic experience, and their significance and value, have been the special preoccupation of philosophers in the Western world since at least the time of Plato. Like other domains within philosophy, one of the primary characteristics of aesthetic theory is the reality that there are serious discussions about, and disagreements over, how art objects and aesthetic experiences are to be interpreted and understood. The articulation of valuative reference points for the arts in particular has generated important debates about the nature of the arts and aesthetic appreciation. The proper place or role of the arts and aesthetic experience, and their connection to other domains and values, also continues to be debated. Such discussions have apparently occupied virtually every period of history, with artists, politicians, critics, and members of a wide array of art audiences expressing positions on the nature of the arts and aesthetics and the value of specific works of art.

It is a truism, but an important one, that art of one sort or another has been highly valued by the array of cultures in which it is found. In spite of differing artistic perspectives and continuing issues in aesthetic theory, virtually everyone would applaud the vitality and meaning of some art forms. Indeed the very term "art" is often used honorifically, to indicate something of creative value, durability, and lasting import. Typically, when an object is designated a "genuine work of art," its status is in some way enhanced, whatever the criteria that led to that designation. It has often been remarked that the arts embody the highest achievements of an age, a society, or a group. Apparently, in spite of significant philosophical differences about its particular value or meaning, then, art of one sort or another is typically seen as an important aspect of a culture that should be preserved and encouraged.

The sense of approbation surrounding art is reflected in contemporary American culture as well. As a society we spend increasing amounts of money watching, listening to, and otherwise interacting with artistic mediums.[1] Many U.S. corporations spend large sums of money in support of the arts, which are increasingly available to the public.[2] Television, film, literature, music, and painting seem to be available to greater numbers of people in our society, and at lower costs. In many ways the contemporary cultural landscape appears to offer a supportive environment for the development and appreciation of art, one in which its value might be readily acknowledged and respected.

That this is not the case, or at least not uniformly so, in all American social and cultural institutions points to a central ambiguity that is a central concern of this chapter. While many people in U.S. society support art with considerable rhetorical flourish, and in spite of the fact that one or another form of art is often accessible, its value and significance for members of our culture, or U.S. society as a whole, are not so clear. The role of art in our public schools is, as well, somewhat problematic. Faced with cost increases and revenue shortfalls, school administrators may find the arts to be a ready avenue for budget reductions. When discussions are held within times of fiscal uncertainty, the arts are sometimes referred to as "frills" whose elimination is justified by that inferior status. Beyond such special circumstances, the rhetorical support that we avow as a culture for art is not always reflected in the realities of everyday school practice, where art may be taught at weekly or longer intervals by teachers whose primary interests and forms of expertise lie elsewhere, included as an elective and therefore considered less essential than other curricular areas, or encouraged as a species of play. The actual practice of art and aesthetic education in schools does not always correspond to the lofty view of art that we, like virtually all cultural groups, seem to entertain.

To understand the predicament facing the arts in American life, and in schools, we must look closely at the traditions in aesthetic theory that we have inherited. By looking at the tenets of those traditions, and how they have helped shape our understanding of the arts, we may begin to recognize the current contradictions in which art is caught. Connecting those crosscurrents with some dominant Western and American cultural, economic, and political tendencies will also be helpful in understanding the place of the arts in daily life. A recognition of the source of these contradictions will also point to philosophical and social changes that are needed in order for art to be a personally, socially, and morally significant cultural force.

Attitudinal Approaches to the Arts

As suggested already, there are few philosophical questions older than those concerned with the nature of "art" and its defining characteristics. Departing from the concerns of ancient philosophers,[3] the advent of a more individualistic and scientific modern age gave credence to assumptions that were quite different from previous understandings of art, understandings that emphasized the discovery of an artistic "essence." Instead, the dispositions or state of mind of the aesthetic participant would come to govern and define the status and possibility of art. The historic movement away from an emphasis on the "art object," toward a focused attention on the "aesthetic experience," can be understood as a concern for the quality of empirical experiences that are made possible through guided perceptual interaction with an object as opposed to a concern to discover its internal essence.

However, the possibility that art might be considered more holistically, as giving rise to experiences that provide insights into general human concerns and interests, became thwarted as attention shifted to various psychological constraints that were to govern our interactions with the arts. A central factor involved in this thwarting of holism, and a divorce of the aesthetic from other, allegedly more mundane, experiences, was the emergence of "attitude theories" of aesthetic experience.[4]

The term "aesthetic" itself is derived from the Greek αεθεσισ (aesthesis), meaning "perception." The first modern attempt to coin the term "aesthetic," and to understand its relationship to other areas, was contained in the work of the German Rationalist, Alexander Gottlieb Baumgarten.[5] His earliest work on this topic, translated as *Reflections*, was an attempt to analyze how "aesthetics is to be the science which will investigate perception for the purpose of describing the kind of perfection which is proper to it. It will have its counterpart in the science of logic which will perform the same office for thought."[6] Baumgarten claims that perception as a form of cognition carries with it a kind of autonomy; his efforts were directed at developing "the principles of a science proper to it."[7] The first modern definition of the aesthetic is provided by Baumgarten at the end of his treatise: "As our definition is at hand, a precise designation can easily be devised. The Greek philosophers and the Church fathers have already carefully distinguished between *things perceived* and *things known*. It is entirely evident that they did not equate *things known* with things of sense, since they honored with this name things also removed from sense (therefore, images). Therefore, *things known* are to be known by the superior faculty as the object of logic; *things perceived* are to be known by the inferior faculty, as the object of the science of perception, or aesthetic."[8] This conferring of autonomy on the aesthetic realm marks the greatest contribution that Baumgarten makes to the modern understanding of the field of aesthetics, and to the appreciation of aesthetic objects. Through this analysis, the aesthetic becomes a discrete, albeit inferior, area of inquiry, distinguishable from other cognitive domains and functions. Less accepted, and hence less successful, was his view that a "science of perception" could be built around the domain of the aesthetic so as to create an epistemology that could rival logic or scientific empiricism.

The dislocation of the aesthetic from other domains is extended by Kant in his classical text, *The Critique of Judgment*.[9] In describing our experience with objects, Kant says that "the satisfaction which we combine with the representation of the existence of an object is called 'interest.'"[10] Yet where a question arises as to whether something is beautiful, Kant argues that we "do not want to know whether anything depends or can depend on the existence of the thing . . . but how we judge it by mere observation. . . ."[11] In addition, Kant continues, "in saying it is beautiful and in showing that I have taste, I am concerned, not with that in which I depend on the existence of the object, but with that which I make out of this representation in myself. . . . Everyone must admit that a judgment about beauty, in which the least interest mingles, is very partial and is not a pure judgment of taste. We must not be in the least prejudiced in favor of the existence of the things, but be quite indifferent in this respect, in order to play the judge in things of taste."[12] In viewing what we see and deciding whether it may justifiably be called beautiful, we are not to be concerned with whether what we see actually exists. Further, if "interest" in the sense Kant uses it involves "the satisfaction which we combine with the representation of the existence of an object," it becomes clear that beauty is not a matter of having an interest in the representation of a real object; or, if such an interest is at work, we cannot be adequate judges of taste.

Basing our perspective on the value of some work insofar as we consider whether it actually exists, or if it excites some interest that "infiltrates" our perception, will result in a partial, and clearly inferior, judgment.

Within attitudinal approaches to aesthetics generally, we are not to be concerned with whether the object actually exists, or how it exists, but only with the perceptual properties of that representation and how they are interpreted. Those properties provide all that is important, as long as our personal interests do not lead us astray. The separation of the aesthetic articulated by Baumgarten is thus enhanced by Kant's insistence on the disconnectedness and autonomy of judgments of taste.

A more extended analysis of the concept of disinterestedness will further clarify the ways in which aesthetic experiences have become separated from other realms of human experience. Lord Shaftesbury has been credited with founding "the first really comprehensive and independent philosophy of the beautiful," and with being the dominant figure in eighteenth century British aesthetics.[13] Jerome Stolnitz, in his discussion of Shaftesbury's contributions to aesthetics, suggests that he "sets into motion the idea which, more than any other, marks off modern from traditional aesthetics and around which a great deal of modern thought has evolved, viz., the concept of 'aesthetic disinterestedness.'"[14]

Disinterestedness is often associated with moral judgment and ethical conduct. "Interest" may refer to what is good for individuals or a society in some normative sense—e.g., when we say that it is in the interest of individuals to treat each other with respect and in the interest of society to create a judicial system that is nondiscriminatory.[15] This sense of "interest" does not depend on what a given individual actually desires. The other sense of "interest" is related to what people take seriously or give their assent to as being personally beneficial, whether or not that is actually the case; this sense of "interest" involves some disposition or inclination on the part of the person involved. Thus, what may be in our normative interest, as a positive value or virtue, may not be desired or even understood by a particular individual. As well, what we find appealing or engaging as a matter of personal interest may not be in our normative interest.

Decisions about what course of action to follow are often made on the basis of what will be most personally advantageous for the person involved, as he or she considers the situation on the basis of self-interest. Such self-interested decisions, though, are at least sometimes superceded by efforts to undertake actions in spite of the possible peril that could result. A person who dashes in front of a moving car that is about to hit a pedestrian, and thus saves that person's life, is sometimes described as being "disinterested," in the sense that he or she does not consider his or her own self-interest before taking action to prevent the accident.

Disinterestedness can refer more generally to an act or experience that is impersonal in the sense that we do not consider human agency or personal proclivities in any particular direction or respect—that is, when we do not calculate the consequences of a particular act. Disinterestedness in this view would lead to activities that would be valuable in and of themselves, or for the value of that action itself, where the possible outcomes or consequences of those activities are not even part of the person's consciousness.

Turning from the domain of personal action to the domain of aesthetic perception, disallowing an appreciation of consequences would essentially mean that the aesthetic "cannot be disinterested unless the spectator forsakes all self-concern and therefore trains attention upon the object for its own sake."[16] Aesthetic perception ought, then, to be focused on, not because of the way that it coincides with our personal interests, nor for the effects that it may bring to us or the society generally, but simply because of the inherent excellence of the art object or aesthetic experience itself. The observer must, then, open himself/herself to the inherent qualities of the object, so that attention and energy can be trained solely on the object. Thus, "to perceive disinterestedly is to make oneself a pure, unflawed mirror, prepared to receive without distortion 'all the impressions, which the objects that are before us can produce.'"[17] The participant in an aesthetic encounter is, therefore, perhaps like nothing so much as a single-minded, but personally empty vessel into which is poured the inherent qualities and characteristics of the object.

Psychical Distance and Aesthetic Value

To develop the kind of focused attention required for a disinterested, bracketed view of an aesthetic object, we must somehow psychologically distance ourselves from the work or experience before us. This basically involves putting the object "out of gear" with our other interests and actions, so that it is not connected to "practical concerns." The basic presumption here is that any art object of symbolic interest—even one that would normally signal danger, fear, or some other emotionally charged reaction—can be approached and appreciated aesthetically if we disconnect it from our usual affections and expectations. To be engaged in a truly aesthetic experience, therefore, we must dislocate our usual way of attending to events, bracketing our typical dispositions, proclivities, and more encompassing social and physical contexts. In accomplishing this dislocation, we will be able to see art "as it is"—unclouded by personal sensibilities and predispositions. A seminal essay that advocates this perspective is Edward Bullough's "'Psychical Distance' as a Factor in Art and an Aesthetic Principle."[18]

In describing the insertion of psychical distance as a way of generating aesthetic experiences, the author asks us to consider a fog at sea. Such a situation is, of course, likely to produce a certain amount of anxiety in passengers. Yet Bullough suggests that a fog at sea can also be a source of pleasure or delight for passengers who have the proper outlook: "abstract from the experience of the sea fog, for the moment, its danger and practical unpleasantness; direct the attention to the features 'objectively' constituting the phenomenon . . . And the experience may acquire, in its uncanny mingling of such concentrated poignancy and delight as to contrast sharply with the blind and distempered anxiety of its other aspects."[19] Rather than anxiety, experiencing a fog at sea can be a source of sensory enjoyment—but only if we are able to insert a kind of distance, bracketing our more usual emotional responses. Such distancing is possible by "putting the phenomenon, so to speak, out of gear with our practical, actual self—by allowing it to stand outside the context of our personal needs and ends—in short, by looking at it 'objectively.'"[20] The insertion of psychological distance into our encounter with empirical events and objects has both positive and negative aspects. In the negative sense, distancing requires that we inhibit our more usual, practical response to situations.

The creation of psychical distance also has a positive dimension, leading to an accentuation of whatever qualities the experience contains vis-à-vis the insertion of this metaphorical distance.

This again serves to distinguish aesthetic experience from our more typical, day-to-day activities and exchanges. By distancing our affections and normal responses to events and objects, we see even common objects in a new way: "The sudden view of things from their reverse, usually unnoticed way, comes upon us as a revelation, and such revelations are precisely those of Art. In this most general sense, Distance is a factor in all Art."[21]

On the view being discussed here, it is clear that aesthetic contemplation is different from our more typical perceptual experiences. What Bullough adds to the previous discussion of the place of aesthetic experience is a psychological element. What is required of those who take part in aesthetic experiences is the separation of their affective tendencies and responses from their perceptual understandings, so that the objective properties of the object can become manifest and, in a significant way, control those experiences. We are, in essence, instructed to put in check our typical response patterns so that they won't interfere with our "unclouded" perception of the inherent qualities of an object viewed aesthetically. It may be surmised here that the insertion of psychical distance, if not a prerequisite for disinterestedness, at least makes the attainment of the latter way of directing experience more likely. The disinterested contemplation of aesthetic phenomena becomes much more assured when we are able to put such phenomena "out of gear with" our practical needs and interests. There is a conceptual tie between disinterestedness and psychical distance.

The specific sort and depth of psychical distance that is required or desirable in a given instance is, Bullough says, difficult to anticipate. Yet a general rule is implicitly offered that is important for understanding attitudinal theories of aesthetic experience in general. He says that works of art that make reference to "organic affections," especially in sexual matters, lie normally below the "Distance-limit." Furthermore, "Allusions to social institutions of any degree of personal importance—in particular, allusions implying any doubt as to their validity—the questioning of some generally recognized ethical sanctions, references to topical subjects occupying public attention at the moment, and such like, are all dangerously near the average limit and may at any time fall below it, arousing, instead of aesthetic appreciation, concrete hostility or mere amusement."[22] The tendency for psychical distance to evaporate within aesthetic encounters requires the artist to proceed carefully; where certain kinds of subject matter may require difficult acts of distancing, they "can be touched upon by Art only with special precautions."[23]

The phenomenon of psychical distance as developed by Bullough provides another important clue in understanding attitudinal theories of aesthetic experience. We are to disengage our actual, practical self when viewing and responding to objects aesthetically, so that we contemplate them unencumbered by our normally attendant affections and interests, which would undermine the search for an "objective" understanding of the qualities inherent in that work. In creating such a perspective on the arts and aesthetic experience, the movement toward viewing works of art as inherently valuable is furthered, just as it is when we adopt the view that disinterested perception is to guide our interaction with art. Psychical distance and disinterestedness both push us in the direction of separating aesthetic experience from our other involvements, perceptions, and actions.

Characteristic of attitude theorists of aesthetic experience, Roman Ingarden discusses the nature of aesthetic value in this way: "The value of an aesthetic object is not the value of a means leading to an end. It is not something which may be ascribed to the object with regard to some objects or states of things existing *outside* it, but it is something *contained in the object itself* and based on the qualities and the harmony of qualities of the aesthetic object itself."[24] For the tradition being examined here, aesthetic experiences are necessarily emotional/psychic ones, distinct from intellectual or cognitive ones. They involve paradigmatically the appreciation of harmonious, inherent qualities, often brought out by an initial excitement provided by a particular aspect of those qualities. We must attend to the qualities of the object or event that we personally distance, if we are to understand the inherent worth of that object. Aesthetic experiences are not to be valued for something they might lead to—whether a desired state of mind or social activity.

This focus on the perceptual, distanced qualities of aesthetic experiences also serves to provide an ontological place for art. Jerome Stolnitz, for example, says that, "works of art can be studied and valued in many ways–morally, as social document, and so on. When we approach the work as a sociologist or moralist, we do not grasp its intrinsic value. To do so we must look at the work without any preoccupation with its origins and consequences. Therefore analysis of such perception is prerequisite to explanation of the *aesthetic* (not the historical, moral, etc.) value of art and the *aesthetic* senses of the term 'beauty.' "[25] To look at and attend to the intrinsic value of art work, thus, we must first dissociate the historical and social forces which attend its creation, and disregard the social and moral consequences of its contemplation. The "art for art's sake" movement of the nineteenth century is an expression of such views and perspectives, carried to their logical conclusion. In the end, adopting this perspective on aesthetic phenomena has serious consequences for those who seek encounters with the aesthetic: "The aesthetic experience, at its best, seems to isolate us and the object from the flow of experience. The object, in being admired for itself, is divorced from its interrelations with other things. And we feel as though life had suddenly been arrested, for we are absorbed wholly in the object before us and abandon any thought of purposive activity looking toward the future."[26]

The views described thus far have helped inform and articulate a modern idea of aesthetic experience that places emphasis on attitudinal, psychological states what are allegedly prerequisite for genuinely aesthetic responses. The effect of this body of writing has been to abstract aesthetic experience from our more usual or ongoing experiences, giving it a life of its own. Such a view places the aesthetic in a realm within which action and conduct are peculiarly irrelevant: "Art . . . is an expression and a stimulus of the imaginative life, which is separated from actual life by the absence of responsive action. Now this responsive action implies in actual life moral responsibility. In art we have no such moral responsibility—it presents a life freed from the binding necessities of our actual existence."[27] A separate universe of experience has been created for objects with which our participation is to be described as aesthetic. Such ideas have, for many, become embedded in our collective sensibilities regarding art and the aesthetic. In letting these become part of our conventional wisdom about interacting with art, however, we must inquire not only into the adequacy or cogency of such aesthetic theories, but into their political, ethical, and ideological implications as well.

One consequence of the aesthetic attitude tradition is a central emphasis on the *perceptual* qualities or the empirical realities contained within works of art. This means that we should see an art object as an end in itself and train attention on the perceptible qualities that it displays. As one writer has expressed this point, "On occasion we pay attention to a thing simply for the sake of enjoying the way it looks or sounds or feels. This is the 'aesthetic' attitude of perception."[28] The art object becomes individuated and autonomous, cut off from connections with other objects, people, and events. It is, in short, an island unto itself.

This emphasis on the perceptual elements of art leads naturally to another manifestation of modern aesthetic theory. In governing our attention to art objects so that their autonomy is ensured, we are drawn to the internal qualities and structures of the art object under observation—e.g., the qualities of shading, color, brush stroke, contrast, etc., in painting. In an important sense this is the only domain still open to us as appreciators, since seeking to understand how the art object may be connected to personal sentiments, social values, and future aims is not permissible when people take the proper aesthetic attitude. Instead, people are to focus on "the looks of things" in aesthetic encounters. "What makes appreciation aesthetic," one writer asserts, "is that it is concerned with a thing's looking somehow without concern for whether it really is like that; beauty we may say, to emphasize the point, is not even skin deep."[29] An abiding interest in an object's form, and the appearance of various schools of Formalism, is a natural outgrowth of the aesthetic attitude.[30]

Attitudinal theories of aesthetic experience remove art—through the development of a particular way of perceiving and understanding sensory input from art objects—from historical and social contexts. Such theories place the appreciator's past and future ideas, experiences, and actions outside the realm of aesthetic contemplation. "Art" on this theory names an abstracted, autonomous, purified domain. Perhaps no single passage in the history of aesthetic theory better captures this point of view than the following, often cited words of Clive Bell: "To appreciate a work of art we need bring with us nothing from life, no knowledge of its ideas and affairs, no familiarity with its emotions. Art transports us from the world of man's activity to a world of aesthetic exaltation. For a moment we are shut off from human interests; our anticipation and memories are arrested; we are lifted above the stream of life."[31] While we may be tempted to think of these remarks as mere hyperbole, they are in keeping with the central tenets of modern aesthetic theory. They represent the pursuit of art as a special, removed, untainted arena, the mysteries of which are accessible only to those with the proper set of dispositional tendencies.

The somewhat abstract ideas and treatises that prompted the development of the aesthetic attitude tradition are, it must be noted, not the exclusive province of aestheticians. The development of programmatic directions in aesthetic and art education has also been influenced by modern aesthetic theory. For example, we can understand the perspective of Harry Broudy as being informed by the ideas discussed in this chapter when he says that our experience of art involves only "the realm of appearance for its own sake, [and consequently] demands no commitment to action."[32] Broudy also cautions that "it is naive to believe that art cannot endanger morals. It can if the viewer is unable to perceive art objects aesthetically, and the untrained perceiver is likely to have this infirmity."[33] Clearly, on this view, art is to be kept safe from the possible taint of politics, social life, and moral imperatives.

As we shall see, this theoretical tradition has been challenged from a variety of perspectives, and on several grounds. Yet it is the understanding of art—its value and significance—that grows out of this tradition that must be analyzed. Attitude theories, in accentuating the presentational, distanced, formal qualities of art, reduce our attention to the surface features of the object while trivializing its content and collapsing its meaning. Moreover, the employment of the ideas contained in modern aesthetic theory has supported the view that the fine or "high" arts are the province of an elite. Not a part of the ebb and flow of human and social experience, art becomes something to behold and focus on during special occasions, in contexts removed from daily life, utilizing a form of attention that makes the domain of art by definition "impractical" and intimidating for many. Art enjoyed through the lenses provided by attitude theories becomes rather easily appropriated by those social groups with the requisite leisure, wealth, and some elusive (and often snobbishly forwarded) dimension of "taste."

A study by Laura Chapman highlights the elitist nature of "the fine arts" in contemporary American culture during the late 1970s.[34] She reports that the median income of those who visited art museums was some $3,500 higher than the national average, while for opera goers the differential was $6,500.[35] Similar discrepancies are reported with respect to the educational level of the art audience.[36] There exists, in short, a "cultural elite," whose income, status, and education clearly demarcate its members. The view of art as an abstracted, isolated, socially and personally ephemeral phenomenon, mandating the creation of a peculiar set of psychological propensities, certainly contributes to the sense that "art" is for the privileged and advantaged. An absorption in the phenomenal field of art works makes artistic appreciation appear not only highly impersonal and abstract, but essentially a matter of discovering appropriate mechanisms of aesthetic sensitivity through the cultivation of taste.

Attitude theories of aesthetic experience also emphasize the ability of participants to see and discriminate among various patterns of sounds, colors, movements, and so on, in accordance with a particular aesthetic medium, and perhaps with the elements of the medium that created those patterns. For example, when analyzing a painting, great attention is placed on the use of different colors and hues, brush strokes, contrasts, symmetry, and so on within the painting itself. Such elements of paintings are central for artists and observers alike, as they constitute the medium through which the aesthetic image is communicated and as they affect the interpretations of the connoisseur. Within the tradition analyzed here, however, the participant in the aesthetic experience has a significantly reduced role, with a correspondingly narrowed range of interpretations regarding the purpose, meaning, and value of the work of art under consideration.

An emphasis on "the looks of things" that accompanies this approach to aesthetic experiences has significantly influenced our notion of aesthetic concepts and meanings. As one writer in aesthetics has argued, "If a thing looks to have a characteristic which is a desirable one from another point of view, its looking so is a proper ground of aesthetic appreciation."[37] Qualities of experience directly available to perception have been labeled by aestheticians as comprising the "sensuous surface" of our world, and they provide the substance for elucidating aesthetic concepts.[38]

On the other hand, the view that a sensuous surface forms the basis for aesthetic concepts does not exhaust the possibility for the development of such concepts. In delimiting what counts as an instance of aesthetic experience via the proper application of the aesthetic attitude, an implicit or explicit claim regarding aesthetic value is being made. Our perception of an object, as an instantiation of aesthetic experience governed by a particular set of constraints, is to be valued because it is an experience of a certain sort—namely, an aesthetic one, governed by the ideas and perspectives discussed above. And such experiences are to be valued as one species of experience that human beings are capable of creating and experiencing.

A literary example provides an instance of this kind of experience. In discussing the reading of poetry, Eliseo Vivas says that "by approaching a poem in a non-aesthetic mode it may function as history, social criticism, as diagnostic evidence of the author's neuroses, and in an indefinite number of other ways."[39] On this view, a work of art is only a work of art if and when it is perceived in a certain way—when, that is, the work becomes the source of an aesthetic experience. For that experience to be possible, the appreciator must adopt the aesthetic attitude. Biographical information about the artist who created that work, daydreaming while ostensibly attending to the elements of it, appreciating it for its historical relevance, and so on, are thus excluded as possibilities of *aesthetic* experience and appreciation. "The aesthetic" forms its own distinctive experience and is not to be confused or conflated with other kinds of undertakings.

Given this focus on the perceptual qualities of art objects that are governed by the adoption of the aesthetic attitude, we should not be surprised that fine art has been characterized as "a selection, refinement, and vivification of intrinsic attention of perceptible unities or forms."[40] Unlike more everyday or "real" empirical objects that compose day-to-day life and that are usually experienced haphazardly, accidentally, incompletely, and with little in the way of an articulated structure that frames conscious perception, art works transcend these qualities to produce a more coherent, unified experience focusing on their intrinsic qualities.

A summary of many of these points can be found in the work of Monroe Beardsley. He suggests that there is wide consensus about what constitutes a valuable aesthetic experience. There is apparent agreement that our attention is to be fixed upon "the components of a phenomenally objective field"; that "it is an experience of some intensity" and one that "hangs together, or is coherent, to an unusually high degree"; and that it is an experience "that is unusually complete in itself."[41] More informatively, the author contends:

> Aesthetic objects have a peculiar, but I think important, aspect: they are all, so to speak, *objets manqués*. There is something lacking in them that keeps them from being quite real, from achieving the full status of things—or, better, that prevents the question of reality from arising. They are complexes of qualities, surfaces. . . . The dancer gives us the abstraction of human action . . . the gestures and movements of joy and sorrow, of love and fear—but not the actions (killing or dying) themselves. This is one sense of "make-believe" in which aesthetic objects are make-believe objects; and upon this depends their capacity to call forth from us the kind of admiring contemplation, without any necessary commitment to practical action, that is characteristic of aesthetic experience.[42]

Since aesthetic objects are not "real," their value cannot be determined vis-à-vis their place among other real objects. Instead, they must be judged on the basis of the kind of experience they produce in their participants. Accordingly, for Beardsley, we must ground aesthetic judgments in a particular kind of phenomenal framework—specifically, using the variables of unity, intensity, and complexity. The use of these categories to make judgments of aesthetic quality presuppose the adoption of the aesthetic attitude and a focus on a phenomenal field, which are among the central topics of this chapter.

The notion that aesthetic experiences are possible only when the object before us is not real and can be understood only in terms of the phenomenal field that is bracketed by disinterestedness, psychical distance, and its internal qualities imposes particular constraints on the percipient and serves to distinguish between the arts and other domains.

The distinction between the "fine arts" and the "popular arts," and especially the development of forms of popular culture, is based in large part on the way that we think about and comprehend the objects and events that we experience and how we understand their nature, purposes, and value. In articulating a disinterested aesthetic, a hierarchy has been promoted within which the fine arts enjoy a superordinate position compared with forms of popular culture. Whether that hierarchy is appropriate or beneficial, however, must be for now an open question. But we do need to ask serious questions about various aspects of modern aesthetic theory and the experiences it generates. In particular, is this approach to the arts and aesthetic value adequate or defensible? Is the aesthetic theory incorporated in this tradition sufficient—and if so, sufficient for *what*?

In cautioning us that images, symbolic representations, and surface qualities of art objects are not identical with actual events and lived circumstances, aestheticians urge us to focus on the perceptible qualities of a painting, for example, and to take account of their phenomenal properties and qualities (like Beardsley's emphasis on unity, intensity, and complexity). In some ways that caution is reasonable, and even important, though it's unlikely that most people above a certain age would be susceptible to that confusion. At a deeper level, though, the bracketing of aesthetic experiences leads often to a diminution of aesthetic quality and value. By bracketing our perception in ways that separate contemplation from action, that lead us to pay attention to art only for the time that we experience and reflect on the object before us, the arts become more peripheral, more temporary, and less given to the pursuit of, and reflection on, substantive aspects of human understanding, social experience, and personal and collective action.

The type of attention paid to the arts within a given group will depend in part on the traditions, ways of life, cultural realities, and other contexts that inform people's understandings of what is possible and desirable. Even larger domains related to patterns of thinking or assumed traditions, political perspectives, and economic realities will affect what is normal, good, and productive. We now turn, hence, to a discussion of how certain cultural and social values in industrial, capitalistic, Western societies are related to an appreciation of the arts.

Technicism and Instrumental Rationality

Technicism is often spoken of in the same breath as technology, and indeed both words share the same root. Yet technicism refers not only to things—high-tech instruments, computers, advanced machinery making space exploration possible, and the like—but to an attitude, a way of organizing life, or a particular worldview. As a worldview, technicism has infiltrated many aspects of American culture that might at first glance seem resistant to it.

One historical aspect of technicism as a way of organizing experience has to do with its utility as a form of control in the workplace. By establishing certain procedures and processes that regulated work, controls could be instituted that would both increase efficiency and protect the interests of those in positions of power. As Richard Edwards has described this, "Technical control emerged from employers' experiences in attempting to control the production (or blue-collar) operations of the firm. The assembly line came to be the classic image, but the actual application of technical control was much broader. Machinery itself directed the labor process and set the pace. . . . Inside the firm, technical control turned the tide of conflict in their [employers'] favor, reducing workers to attendants of prepared machinery."[43] Thus technicism as a way of organizing and controlling work affected the way people came to think about themselves, their fellow workers, and their role in the workplace.

Such forms of control gradually extended their influence, becoming accepted by many as cultural constraints that influenced ways of life, thus touching a range of daily practices. As Christopher Lasch has commented, a mode of domination became more encompassing: "Much advanced technology embodies by design (in both senses of the word) a one-way system of management and communication. It concentrates economic and political control—and, increasingly, cultural control as well—in a small elite of corporate planners, market analysts, and social engineers. . . . Technology thus comes to serve as an effective instrument of social control [for example] . . . by presenting the choice of leaders and parties as a choice among consumer goods."[44] Technicism, in short, involves the ability of some segment of society to "impersonally" or "naturally" control the choices that are then presented to others, in the process maintaining a disparity of power that can effect political, social, and cultural practices and values.

Technicism is also closely associated with the development of instrumental reason. This involves an emphasis on developing particular, specialized, often dehumanizing means to efficiently engineer the emergence of a desired end. The result is an obsession with techniques that can be employed in the accomplishment of an end that, by and large, remains beyond critique.[45] Instrumental rationality thus centers on the location, and implementation, of those behaviors that will bring about some desired endpoint in the most expeditious (quickest, least expensive, with fewest harmful side effects, etc.) way. Connecting this form of rationality with Lasch's point about the manipulative qualities of technicism, it is important to see that this way of thinking tends to separate those who conceptualize desired endpoints from those who carry out the related, instrumental activities that will lead to them. This separation is seen, for example, in most economic institutions in U.S. society, where a few people conceptualize the desirable ends of manufacturing while the rest of us perform actions to help realize them, using the appropriate methods and techniques.

At a more philosophical level, technical and instrumental reason have an affinity with the dominance of positivism within the natural and social sciences. Bredo and Feinberg describe this: "Logical positivism . . . served to bring together two very powerful bases for knowledge: an empiricism that based knowledge on sensory or observational experience and a rationalism that based knowledge on self-evidently clear and consequential arguments. Logic became the scaffolding on which one modeled the world, while the facts of sensory or observational experience provided the constraints to which the logical model had to conform . . . logical positivism was in a strong position to legitimize itself as *the* paradigm for true knowledge of the world."[46] In incorporating the twin pillars of true, unconditional, secure knowledge—clear empirical observations and logical/mathematical deductions—positivism asserted its preeminence over other claims to genuine knowledge. Statements could be proven either by appeal to their analytic truth (i.e., statements that are true given the definitions of the terms used) or in virtue of their correspondence to empirical realities. In both the natural and social sciences, positivism was seen by many as the guiding light in the location of justifiable methods and certain results.

The empirical truths associated with positivism were to be located in the methods of the natural sciences. As the foundation for empirical knowledge, our assertions must be grounded in observable facts that are dissociated from values and personal predilections; hence we see the historical development of the fact/value dichotomy in the sciences. A scientist's findings, as the epitome of such knowledge, must be purely factual, based on observations and calculations that are objective, universal, and value-free. Moreover, it must be possible to replicate the findings of one set of experiments, so that conclusions or hypotheses may be confirmed or falsified in other investigations. Given sufficient observations and related scientific theories, laws may be identified that acknowledge the regularity of natural processes. By basing findings exclusively on factual data, carefully controlling for extraneous variables that may skew scientific procedures, developing lawful generalizations, and displacing the realms of judgment, value, and emotion, irrefutable knowledge may be provided. One of the central consequences of positivism is its displacement or derogation of other forms of inquiry, research, and knowledge. Given a reliance on analytic and empirical truths, proponents of positivism deny the validity of metaphysical, valuative, and social undertakings for which the necessary regularity and precision are apparently not forthcoming. In rejecting valuative inquiry, such as that involved in aesthetics and ethics as a source of knowledge, an epistemological hierarchy, and the methods to acquire it, are established.

Positivism as it emphasizes methodological strictures thus underlines our culture's obsession with the technical and instrumental as neutral, value-free, procedural activities helping to accomplish some end. The fact that modern science has been so concerned with the preservation of "*the* scientific method" is thus no accident.[47] While maintaining control through the development of a hierarchy of power, technicism reassures us that the results obtained will be objective, value-free, and justifiable. Thus a faith in experts, who have command of techniques that are ostensibly removed from self-interest, and who base their conclusions solely on factual realities and inductive reasoning, is appropriate; at the same time, technical manipulation and instrumental reason are utilized to maintain the experts' superordinate, controlling positions.

Commodification and Mass Production

Commodification refers to one of the central planks in the economic platform on which our culture is partly constructed. While this tendency, like the phenomenon of technicism, involves a complex set of ideas, what it basically refers to is this: Our economy is organized around the production of goods that can be entered into and distributed through a system of markets. The desired end of a production system, of course, is the largest production of goods at the lowest price, with a corresponding increase in profit accumulation. Given these basic tenets of capitalism, various measures may be introduced to make the manufacturing process more efficient,[48] the sales of goods more widespread, and the outlay of capital within the manufacturing process less extensive.

The status of goods produced within this system, more generally, undergoes an important transformation that is related to the status of art within American culture. Instead of capturing and exemplifying the personal, communal, and even moral sensibilities associated with a genuine craft, goods are produced that to a significant extent lie beyond the interests and ideas of the producers. As work becomes more mechanized, fragmented, and routine, with workers having less control over the total process of production, the resulting goods embody less and less that is relevant to the identity, character, and personality of the producer. Goods, in short, become *commodities*, packaged, distributed, and sold on some market in an effort to increase the accumulation of capital. No longer is work prized for its intrinsic worth or even for its enjoyment; nor is the product of work seen as embodying something of general value to a person, social group, or community. Instead, its utility in furthering the profitability of the overall business operation defines its value. Within this consumerist orientation, the goods produced decline in terms of what we might call the artistic or aesthetic qualities of craft: those acts, often small, idiosyncratic, and unpredictable in nature, whereby what we produce and how we produce are intimately connected with who we are as a person and a member of a community. Commenting on the more psychological side of this process, Lasch notes that a culture of consumption "dissolves the world of substantial things . . . , replaces it with a shadowy world of images, and thus obliterates the boundaries between the self and its surroundings."[49]

As the drive for the production of "shadowy images" accelerates, various technical devices are advanced to help ensure their low-cost production and widespread distribution; mass production and consumption become the heart of this system. This has major consequences for art. As Walter Benjamin has put it, in a seminal essay on this subject: "The authenticity of a thing is the essence of all that is transmissible from its beginning, ranging from its substantive duration to its testimony to the history which it has experienced. Since the historical testimony rests on the authenticity, the former, too, is jeopardized by reproduction when substantive duration ceases to matter. And what is really jeopardized when the historical testimony is affected is the authority of the object. One might subsume the eliminated element in the term "aura" and go on to say: that which withers in the age of mechanical reproduction is the aura of the work of art."[50] No longer a part of history, tradition, or community, the mechanically reproduced art object loses the authenticity, signature, and contextual value with which it was once ingrained. It is not the meaning of Picasso's *Guernica* that is important, but the fact of having ("owning") a reproduction of that painting per se that is significant within a culture of mass consumption and distribution. Instead of an aesthetic aura, we are left with a semblance of artistic integrity. As a form of exchange, the work of art as commodity constricts what is meaningful about art.

Several social and economic factors have shaped our culture's view of art in potentially debilitating ways. When the arts are embedded within an ethos of technicism, or procured as forms of commodity exchange, their status and value are trivialized. They are reduced in value in terms of a lack of epistemic value, in the first case, and reduced to a form of mercenary exchange, in the second. Subordinate to the traditions of objectivity and certainty in positivism, art can't help but be regarded as an inferior, second-rate phenomenon, though perhaps providing an area of nonserious release from the domain of "genuine knowledge," to be pursued as a form of entertainment (and of play, especially within schools). Within the context of technicism it is not surprising that art is caught in hostile crosscurrents—swept up in images of intellectual inferiority and emotivist emptiness.[51] As a form of commodity exchange, art is isolated from important traditions, histories, and commitments, separated from those human and communal activities from which might be derived an important place for the aesthetic undertaking.

Conclusions

The historic developments that lead to the growth of modern aesthetic theory served to dislocate art from personal insight as well as abstracting it from social and historical contexts. Requiring a complex distancing of psychological and emotional responses to art, linked with a related emphasis on the art object's formal features in and of themselves, the experience of art seems more and more impersonal and remote. The pursuit of an objective aesthetic may well have been purchased at the expense of its significance.

In a similar fashion, the more recent commodification of images and objects within a materialistic culture has led to a reduction in the power of art forms. As works of art become valued for pecuniary reasons, and as mechanical forms of reproduction serve to make aesthetic forms more and more interchangeable, the domain of art loses its legitimacy and power.

In both cases, the aesthetic experience and interactions with particular works of art become less and less personally meaningful. And the lives we lead become as a result increasingly shallow. The remainder of this book is devoted, in large part, to considering ways in which those tendencies can be reversed.

Notes

1. Following are figures from the *National Income and Product Accounts of the United States, 1929–94*: Volume 1 (Washington, DC: Government Printing Office, April 1998): Table 2.4, "Personal Consumption Expenditures by Type of Expenditure, annually, 1929–94. For "Books and maps," figures for selected years are as follows (in billions of dollars): 1950: .7 billion; 1960: 1.1; 1970: 2.9; 1980: 6.5; and 1990 (the most recent year for which data are available): 17.6. For "Video and audio products, computer equipment, and musical instruments," the figures are (in billions of dollars): 1950: 1.1; 1960: 3.1; 1970 8.5; and 1980: 19.9. For "admissions to legitimate theatres and opera, and entertainments of nonprofit institutions (except athletics)," the figures are: 1950: .2; 1960: .3; 1970: .5; and 1980: 1.8. Interestingly, these figures are listed under the heading "Recreation".

2. Following are figures from the *Annual Survey of Corporate Contributions, 1984 Edition* (New York: The Conference Board, Inc., 1984): total corporate contributions to "Culture and Art" were as follows: 1972, $13,980,000 or 4.1% of total corporate giving; 1980: $108,673,000 or 10.9% of corporate giving; 1982 (the latest year for which information has been compiled): $145,838,000 or 11.4% of total corporate giving.

3. See, for example, Rupert C. Lodge, *Plato's Theory of Art* (New York: Russell and Russell, 1975).

4. I use the phrase "attitude theories" generically to cover a variety of specific positions in aesthetics. All of these theories share, however, the view that it is something about the *attitude* of the participant that is definitive of aesthetic experience. For a more detailed account of these theories, see the references cited in footnotes 5 through 9, below.

5. Alexander Gottlieb Baumgarten, *Reflections on Poetry*, translated by Karl Aschenbrenner and William B. Holther (Berkeley: University of California Press, 1954).

6. Ibid., p. 4.

7. Ibid., p. 4.

8. Ibid., p. 78.

9. Immanuel Kant, *Critique of Judgment*, translated by J. H. Bernard (New York: Hafner Publishing Company, 1972).

10. Ibid., p. 38.

11. Ibid., p. 38.

12. Ibid., p. 39.

13. Ernst Cassirer, *The Philosophy of the Enlightenment* (Boston: Beacon Press, 1955), p. 312.

14. Jerome Stolnitz, "On the Significance of Lord Shaftesbury in Modern Aesthetic Theory," *Philosophical Quarterly*, 11, no. 43 (April 1961): p. 107.

15. See Amy Gutmann, *Democratic Education* (Princeton, NJ: Princeton University Press, 1987).

16. Stolnitz, "Lord Shaftesbury," p. 107.

17. Jerome Stolnitz, "On the Origins of 'Aesthetic Disinterestedness," in *Aesthetics: A Critical Anthology*, ed. George Dickie and Richard J. Sclafani (New York: St. Martin's Press, 1977), p. 618.

18. Edward Bullough, "'Psychical Distance' as a Factor in Art and an Aesthetic Principle," *British Journal of Psychology*, 5 (1912): pp. 87–98; reprinted in Dickie and Sclafani, *Aesthetics*, pp. 758–782.

19. Bullough, in Dickie and Sclafani, *Aesthetics*, p. 759.

20. Ibid., p. 759.

21. Ibid., p. 760.

22. Ibid., p. 764.

23. Ibid., p. 764.

24. Roman Ingarden, "Aesthetic Experience and Aesthetic Object," *Philosophy and Phenomenological Research* 21 (1961): pp. 289–313.

25. Jerome Stolnitz, *Aesthetics and Philosophy of Art Criticism* (Boston: Houghton Mifflin Company, 1960), p. 29.

26. Ibid., p. 52.

27. Roger Fry, *Vision and Design* (London: Chatto and Windus Ltd., 1920), excerpted in *Problems in Aesthetics*, ed. Morris Weitz (London: Macmillan Company, 1970), p. 52.

28. Stolnitz, *Aesthetics and Philosophy of Art Criticism*, p. 34.

29. J. O. Urmson, "What Makes a Situation Aesthetic?" in *Contemporary Studies in Aesthetics*, ed. Francis J. Coleman (New York: McGraw-Hill Book Company, 1968).

30. For example, see DeWitt H. Parker, *The Principles of Aesthetics* (Boston: Silver, Burdett, and Co., 1920); Stephen C. Pepper, *Principles of Art Appreciation* (New York: Harcourt, Brace, & World, 1949). Also see Monroe C. Beardsley, *Aesthetics: Problems in the Philosophy of Criticism* (New York: Harcourt, Brace, & World, 1958); and D. W. Gotshalk, *Art and the Social Order* (New York: Dover Publications, 1962).

31. Clive Bell, *Art* (New York: Frederick A. Stokes Co., 1913), p. 25.

32. Harry S. Broudy, *The Whys and Hows of Aesthetic Education* (St. Louis: CEMREL, 1977), p. 7.

33. Harry S. Broudy, *Enlightened Cherishing: An Essay in Aesthetic Education* (Urbana: University of Illinois Press, 1972), p. 48.

34. Laura H. Chapman, *Instant Art, Instant Culture: The Unspoken Policy for American Schools* (New York: Teachers College Press, 1982).

35. Ibid., p. 172.

36. Ibid., p. 172.

37. Urmson, "What Makes a Situation Aesthetic?"

38. D. W. Prall, *Aesthetic Judgment* (New York: Crowell, 1929).

39. Eliseo Vivas, "Contextualism Reconsidered," *Journal of Aesthetics and Art Criticism*, 18 (1959): pp. 224–225.

40. D. W. Gotshalk, *Art and the Social Order* (New York: Dover Publications, 1962), p. 108.

41. Monroe C. Beardsley, *Aesthetics: Problems in the Philosophy of Criticism* (New York: Harcourt, Brace, & World, 1958), p. 528.

42. *Ibid.*, p. 529

43. Richard Edwards, *Contested Terrain: The Transformation of the Workplace in the Twentieth Century* (New York: Basic Books, 1979), p. 20.

44. Christopher Lasch, *The Minimal Self: Psychic Survival in Troubled Times* (New York: W. W. Norton & Company, 1984), p. 26.

45. See William Barrett, *The Illusion of Technique* (New York: Anchor Press, 1978).

46. Eric Bredo and Walter Feinberg, eds., *Knowledge and Values in Social and Educational Research* (Philadelphia: Temple University Press, 1982), p. 14.

47. For an important critique of this position, see Paul K. Feyerabend, *Against Method: Outline of an Anarchistic Theory of Knowledge* (London: Verso Edition, 1978).

48. This was the guiding force behind the investigations of Frederick W. Taylor. See Edwards, *Contested Terrain.*

49. Lasch, *Minimal Self*, p. 52.

50. Walter Benjamin, "The Work of Art in the Age of Mechanical Reproduction," in his *Illuminations*, ed. Hannah Arendt (New York: Schocken Books, 1969), p. 221.

51. On the development of emotivism and its influence in moral theory especially, see Alasdair MacIntyre, *After Virtue* (Notre Dame: University of Notre Dame Press, 1984).

Chapter 2

The Meaning and Significance of Art

There are a number of possible ways to understand, interpret, and critique the views concerning the aesthetic attitude, aesthetic concepts, and aesthetic value that generate the theories discussed in the previous chapter. Criticisms of the aesthetic attitude tradition as this provides a foundation for aesthetic experience are numerous, focusing on one or more of its alleged inadequacies for the philosophy of art and art criticism.[1]

My general aim in this chapter is to provide a critique of the ways in which the arts have been seen and thought about, and the extent to which they have been too narrowly circumscribed, as a result of the perspectives discussed in chapter 1. I am primarily concerned with how certain conceptual issues in philosophical aesthetics have misunderstood the relationship between politics and culture, the arts and meaning, in society and in schools; and how they have constricted the nature of aesthetic value.[2] The ideas and analyses presented below provide reasons for thinking that the picture of the aesthetic experience needs to be broadened in particular ways and show how such a broadened perspective—one that includes the contributions of the popular arts—might affect the meaning of the arts. The critique provided below also suggests how conceptions of the nature of aesthetic experience affect its perceived value, relationships with other activities and experiences, and so on, conceptions that are central for the general purposes of this book. In arguing against the sort of "Presentational Aesthetic" portrayed in the previous chapter, and against some of its curricular derivatives in aesthetic education, I provide an analysis of the ideological and political dimensions of these theories.

The first portion of this chapter outlines the conceptual inadequacies, within the domain of philosophical aesthetics, of attitude theories of aesthetic experience. This involves an analysis and critique of the views of aesthetic concepts and value embedded in this philosophical tradition. The central question here revolves around the extent to which this set of suppositions and assumptions provides an acceptable, adequate, or comprehensive basis on which to understand aesthetic significance and meaning.[3] More specifically, this theory of aesthetic value does not explain the full range of our interactions with aesthetic objects. Nor does it allow for the complete potential of aesthetic experience to be realized.

Closely related to the critique involved in the initial section of this chapter is an analysis of the rather superficial view of aesthetic value, a view which results from these theoretical positions. As I will show in section 2, the inadequacies of this view are a result of the creation of a separate, discrete realm for the aesthetic. Because "aesthetic" and "non-aesthetic" experiences are conceptualized as so disjointed, the relationship of the former to more broadly based human and social concerns and interests is overlooked or disallowed. Put another way, a Presentational Aesthetic—a theory that makes the surface features or presentational qualities of objects and artifacts preeminent as a source of aesthetic value—undermines the possibility of an informing, more interactive relationship between aesthetic experience, personal meaning, and social action.

Having discussed the philosophical shortcomings of attitudinal theories, we will be in a better position to understand the ways in which a Presentational Aesthetic contains at least implicit ideological commitments. These commitments are of special importance in analyzing why particular theories and programs have been promulgated in society as well as in schools.

Shortcomings of Aesthetic Attitude Theories

This analysis and critique centers on the rather narrow conception of aesthetic meaning and significance, a conception that has resulted from the legacy of modern aesthetic theory. The range of possible meanings and levels of significance is as a result unduly restrictive. Nor can attitude theories account for or explain the depth of at least some of our experiences with works of art. This critique requires some preliminary analysis of the concepts of aesthetic meaning and significance.

We can, for heuristic purposes, divide the concepts of meaning and significance in aesthetic experience. "Meaning" refers to efforts at "reading" or making sense of whatever object, situation, or artifact is the source of aesthetic experience, while "significance" refers to the ways in which aesthetic participants are drawn to or moved by that object, or how the experience generates insights or reflections that are illuminating. The concept of aesthetic meaning, then, will pertain to how the work of art is integrated—how its various elements, composition, and so on, work together to help create the opportunity for an experience. Meaning within aesthetic experience refers both to the formal features of the art work—its surface features—and to the content or representational features of the work, including its symbolic content. Generalizing on these points, we may say that the meaning of an aesthetic object refers to the arrangement of the object's formal features, its representational content or structure, as well as the interpretive and symbolic understandings generated by our interaction with that object.

The significance of aesthetic objects, on the other hand, refers to the effect of such objects on the thoughts, dispositions, ideas, feelings, and so on, of the aesthetic participant. Aesthetic significance pertains to the ways in which aesthetic objects convey something of import to the participant, how they add something to the lives of people who experience and appreciate works of art. To speak of the aesthetic significance of objects and artifacts is to get at the very central questions of why we spend both time and energy on their construction and their appreciation and how they affect people outside aesthetic experiences.

Aesthetic attitude theories prescribe how we are to obtain and justify both an object's aesthetic meaning and its significance; indeed, these two categories seem virtually identical. They restrict possible sources of meaning and significance so that only those in accord with certain psychological traits or dispositional constraints are considered legitimate or appropriate. In short, the aesthetic attitude details how we must perceive objects if our interactions with them are to be genuinely aesthetic and, consequently, if the meaning and significance we attach to them is to be authentic. Let us see how the types of interaction sanctioned by this attitude limit the domain of aesthetic meaning and significance.

We can think about the tenets of aesthetic attitude theories as unfolding along a continuum of possible emphases. At one end of this continuum, we can readily see how a strictly interpreted, deeply entrenched aesthetic attitude may result in the Formalist approach represented in the views of Stephen Pepper and DeWitt Parker.[4] On this view the meaning of the aesthetic object is to be directly "read off" the surface features of the object itself: depending on the medium involved, its sound and pitches, colors and lines, or characterization and plot. To be sure, elaborate and extensive categories have been developed within artistic mediums, categories to evaluate these formal properties. Yet not only is the object's meaning to be discovered in such surface features, its significance seems equally limited to the kinds of appreciative exercises inherent in a focused attention on the formal categories that are constructed. The significance of aesthetic experience is in this way restricted to an appreciation of the relationships between the formal features of objects and artifacts. Governed by such a delineation of an object's formal qualities, we may well be puzzled by the vast amounts of time and energy that are devoted to the creation and appreciation of works of art. About all we could reasonably be expected to gain from aesthetic experience of this sort is perhaps a greater sense of discrimination of the formal structures and designs of particular works. We may be better able to distinguish among subtle differences in color, timbre, etc., as a result of such appreciative experiences. But it is difficult to see what significance such experiences could in turn have for the appreciator, or what other value such experiences could contribute to, other than perhaps to increase our formal interaction with still other objects and artifacts (which would of course also be viewed and found significant in this Formalist sense). Now such a process of ever-increasing sensory sophistication or discrimination may be justified if all one is concerned with are the perceptible colors, shapes, sounds, etc., which surround us—i.e., if the significance of art can be understood solely in terms of the surface qualities and interrelationships of particular empirical qualities. Even though developing this sort of perceptual acumen may be beneficial at one level,[5] the lack of attention to other possible meanings and kinds of significance seems to obfuscate just those features that we find powerful or compelling in at least some works of art. The paucity of interpretations associated with the aesthetic attitude may be illustrated by the response we would have, say, to someone who reacted to and discussed only the qualities of line, shading, and shape which inhere in Picasso's *Guernica*. In such a case, while we may admit that the aesthetic participant has gained *something* with respect to sensory perception or discrimination, we would add (probably in the same breath) that our imaginary percipient has experienced only a small fraction of the diverse meanings and insights that this painting is capable of providing; in short, that he/she has missed the significance of Picasso's work. We would doubtless suggest that there is something fundamentally lacking in that person's appreciation of *Guernica* such that it makes sense to say to that person, "You saw *something* (perhaps 'pigments on canvas' or the like), but it wasn't Picasso's work entitled *Guernica*." We might also encourage the viewer to look at the painting again, and suggest how the other insights and perspectives that it contains might be recognized and appreciated. In any case, we can see in this illustration how the kind of interpretive/evaluative activities that take place when one adopts a strictly aesthetic attitude, or Formalist, approach to aesthetic experience results in the disquieting feeling that there is more to works of art than "meets the eye."

At the other end of our hypothesized aesthetic attitude continuum, the injunction to attend only to the discernible properties of objects viewed ahistorically and asocially may be taken as offering a "point of entry" into the aesthetic domain, from which other activities and experiences may be developed or constructed. That is, identifying and appreciating perceptible qualities in objects and artifacts may be a starting block from which one's experiences are enlarged upon and intermingled. Further, understanding the importance of an *aesthetic* attitude may necessitate realizing the rather different ways in which we customarily see and evaluate objects and events in general, and this realization may itself be of some importance. This approach is in fact given support by attitude theorists who argue that an aesthetic way of perceiving things is importantly different from our more usual, utilitarian or pragmatic frames of reference. The latter emphasis sees people and objects as means to something else considered good or valuable, something to be valued to the extent that they foster or enhance the attainment of those ends. Distinguishing the patterns of attending to the arts as these are shaped by the aesthetic attitude, on one hand, and from a more technical/instrumental perspective on the other hand, may clarify some of the perceptual and ideological problems associated with technicism and positivism discussed at the end of chapter 1. Examples of these different ways of seeing abound. We are accustomed to regarding the value of pens, paper, and word-processing systems as being realized in the way that they allow us to achieve some connected goal or purpose: the communication of ideas, the depiction of events, and so on. While such a utilitarian perspective is often desirable and necessary for certain purposes, proponents of the aesthetic attitude may be seen as arguing that if we pay attention to the qualities of even so mundane an object as a pen or computer, apart from its communicative utility, something of interest about such an object may "appear" or become available to our perceptual awareness. More expansively, in looking at objects in a way that puts them "out of gear" with our more usual mode of perception, we may notice certain features of our environment that would otherwise be invisible. And these features may subsequently lead to an increased sensitivity to and understanding of experiences, objects, and actions, when seen as "ends in themselves" and not as instrumentally useful.

This is an important, if perhaps problematic, insight—in at least three ways. First, this orientation to the aesthetic attitude may in fact illuminate our understanding of at least some experiences by accentuating otherwise hidden dimensions or aspects of them. We may, that is, notice for the first time something about the way common, ordinary objects look or sound or feel, something that adds a level of understanding which has previously been inaccessible. Instead of looking at the "value" of a particular setting in terms of how the site on which it is located might provide a profitable setting for a new shopping center, we may instead notice how the cornices, the angles and pitches of the roof, the arches and cornices that provide the perimeter details of the existing structure, work together in ways that provoke significant aesthetic interest. Thus the meaning of this building may be transformed from a utilitarian, materialistic contemplation of square footage and profitability to a more intrinsically valuable, aesthetically satisfying contemplation of the building's architectural features. Such a reorienting of our awareness and perceptual attention can indeed be illuminating.

Admitting this to be the case, however, a second question is raised that may provide further insight. That question is, What is the significance of this new way of noticing and appreciating the perceptible features of the building? In short, what does it matter, or what ramifications might there be (in our future observations, actions, and outlook) as a result of this way of contemplating the building? We may indeed be struck by and appreciate for the first time the intricacies, architectural details, and workmanship of the building hypothesized above; yet what significance do such appreciative activities themselves possess? It may, of course, be insightful, given the operation of the aesthetic attitude, to notice new things about specific objects. Yet do such perceptions "merely" extend or enliven our future noticings in some way? If so, we must ask, again, if such an orientation isn't missing something of importance about our (potential, at least) interactions with objects and artifacts. And this puts us squarely back in the same dilemma that we saw resulting from the more strict rendering of the aesthetic attitude: Is our interpretation and appreciation of aesthetic objects only directed at the further discrimination of other objects' perceptible qualities, or does some other purpose underlie the effort to refocus attention toward an object's inherent qualities, away from its utilitarian value? The version of the aesthetic attitude under examination here calls attention to an issue which is by now familiar: How can attending to objects via the adoption of an aesthetic attitude be justified and valued?

Thirdly, the fact that an aesthetic attitude is useful in reorienting perception and those attitudes which underlie it says something interesting about our "ordinary" way of looking at things. The "aesthetic attitude" becomes so strained and artificial, in part, because we are so accustomed to thinking and perceiving in utilitarian or pragmatic terms—or to regarding them as commodity forms. If we primarily value an object instrumentally and then become able to consciously view the same object intrinsically, the significance of that revised perception must be understood in the context of our more normal patterns. The aesthetic attitude can be provocative and illuminating, thus, because it entails a perspective that differs so markedly from the way we have come, in normal, everyday exchanges and experiences, to look at ourselves and our everyday world.

The considerations enunciated above point to the inadequacies inherent in the aesthetic attitude tradition, whether this be strictly or loosely interpreted. If strictly interpreted attitude theories result in a kind of Formalism, and loosely interpreted theories produce a view that sees surface elements as but one point of entry into the aesthetic domain, a middle position might be advanced such that, in providing a beginning for aesthetic experience, these surface elements must be the ultimate source of adjudication for competing interpretations. Within such a "middle ground" rendering of the aesthetic attitude, the surface features of aesthetic objects would ultimately determine accurate judgments from inaccurate judgments of aesthetic meaning. Yet the question of the significance of such experiences would remain just as unsettled under this characterization of the aesthetic attitude tradition as it does under the two previously discussed. All three variations, in subscribing to the central tenets of attitudinal approaches to aesthetic experience, fail to satisfactorily explain or account for the depth of significance and persuasiveness of such experience.

Without wanting to completely deny the value of some particular attitude that percipients adopt when attending to aesthetic objects, then, certain core problems seem endemic to such approaches to aesthetic experience. These problems admit of no obvious or clear solution. The first of these is that, in their strict version, aesthetic attitude theories simply do not explain the level of significance—the depth of feeling, emotion, and thought—that is produced by certain art works and other objects and events which are of a particularly profound or moving nature. Attending to only those surface features of a film, painting, or sculpture that we are able to directly perceive, perhaps even with great lucidity and penetration, does not exhaust the possibilities for aesthetic significance. Attending to and making sense of the surface qualities of Coppola's *Apocalypse Now*—even if we are sensitized to the myriad qualities of the film medium—simply does not reveal or disclose the full significance of this work. Such appreciative experiences miss something important about the power or capacities of at least some important art works; it is just those works, works that may be most influential or have the greatest impact on viewers, that seem to be only partially illuminated, at best, by the kind of formal analysis prescribed through modern aesthetic theory.

In addition, what these approaches to aesthetics miss, in a sense, is the *content* of aesthetic experience. Attitudinal approaches to aesthetic experience are virtually devoid of content, leaving the percipient to savor only those presentational features immediately accessible through the adoption of a particular attitude during the actual encounter with the artwork. A sustained analysis of how interpretation, elaboration, and connection with other experiences and events are often important aspects of our interaction with aesthetic objects is disallowed. While perhaps an important part of aesthetic perception at one level, aesthetic attitude theories block other kinds of analyses and approaches which could further develop the meaning and significance of our interactions with such objects.

In sum, what seems to be most lacking in the accounts of aesthetic experience which center on the importance of embracing the correct attitude is, first, an adequate theory of aesthetic meaning, of how an object's formal qualities are related to its subject matter or content and how both the form and content of a work interact in the construction of that meaning. In their more extreme version, aesthetic attitude theories leave out of consideration any elements save the formal features of artifacts and their interrelations; the meaning of a work of art is thus reduced to what we can directly discern in some aseptic sort of perceptual oasis where history, society, and personal inclinations are equally irrelevant. All that is needed to determine an object's aesthetic meaning are those surface features of the medium which construct the physical object. Second, attitude theories constrain what is significant about works of art. They limit the impact of art to that which can be explained by reference to the sensual qualities of the object itself—to the discovery, articulation, and appreciation of whatever formal characteristics it displays. But the question remains: Appreciation and articulation for what? Focusing the viewer's attention on immediately accessible features and discernible sensory qualities, such theories are conceptually incomplete as a framework for understanding and appreciating aesthetic objects. Even in their less strident versions, aesthetic attitude theories are incomplete in their formulation, offering us only one face of the multifarious aspects which compose the aesthetic. While the admonition to examine closely the presentational features of an object is often important and useful, unless accompanied by further investigations, analyses, and interpretations that lie outside the object per se, such admonitions are likely to bear little fruit.

By defining the aesthetic domain so narrowly, even less strictly interpreted attitude theories delimit the nature of aesthetic value to an unreasonable and unnecessary extent. Consider again the example of the building whose aesthetic features would otherwise be overshadowed by a concern for its more utilitarian, materialistic value were it not for the operation of an aesthetic attitude. Certainly something is to be gained by cutting short this kind of technical, commodified orientation and paying attention to the visual and architectural properties of the building itself. Still, only the immediate experience of the building and its presentational qualities are to be of import. Thus our spectator may come to look at, appreciate, and even value the building differently as a result of adopting a less utilitarian perspective. Yet what is the purchase of this altered perception? Where might such enhanced perception lead? Since aesthetic experiences are to be valued intrinsically, the only value this encounter can have is in increasing or refining our sensual awareness of this building's, and perhaps others', formal qualities. While this is not unimportant, there are other possibilities that remain unrealized within such a guiding framework. Consider, for example, the possibility that in seeing the building differently, in apprehending and appreciating its aesthetic features, our spectator is led to value it to the extent that he/she questions the motives that initially led to the plan to have it razed. Aesthetic experiences of a certain sort and intensity can, in this way, cause people to rethink their values, assumptions, and convictions in other areas as well, and to think and act differently as a result. The aesthetic attitude could be seen as initiating people into new ways of thinking, seeing, and understanding, ways that lead them to see themselves, their relations with others, and a diverse array of objects and interests differently.[6]

Yet this is precisely the kind of impact excluded by even the weaker versions of the aesthetic attitude tradition; it is forbidden by the kind of conceptual underpinnings which are core elements of this tradition. In drawing distinct, rigid lines between aesthetic and other kinds of experiences, and in positing an asocial, ahistorical, impersonal sort of abstracted domain governed by a bracketed perception, connections between aesthetic objects and other experiences and actions are effectively eliminated as viable aesthetic possibilities. In admonishing us to value aesthetic objects in and of themselves and to perceive them disinterestedly, in some abstracted, evanescent arena available through a kind of psychological distancing, we are left with a rather impoverished notion of what is of value and significance aesthetically.

Again, this is not to deny the historical and conceptual importance of noticing how aesthetic qualities are different from prudential, pragmatic, or utilitarian ones. Attempts at redirecting our awareness away from the latter concerns (while understanding their social and ideological causes) and toward a more sustained analysis of the object's sensory features are of no small moment. A theory of aesthetic response, meaning, and significance which ends here, however, must be regarded as incomplete and shortsighted.

The Abstracted Nature of a Presentational Aesthetic

The comments in the preceding section begin to raise serious questions regarding the extent to which we can isolate the aesthetic surface of objects from our other experiences and still have a deep sense of aesthetic meaning and significance. Indeed, we must reject the notion that aesthetic attitude theories provide a guiding framework for our interactions with aesthetic objects because they exclude so much from such interactions. Part of the reason for this exclusion is that the aesthetic is seen as occupying a special realm or area, apart from other concerns, interests, social relations and realities, and events. Recall that a crucial component of attitude theories is their insistence that understanding aesthetic objects entails a process of stripping away from our perception those elements that do not directly relate to the presentational qualities of the object. Inherent in this reductionist view are the beliefs that aesthetic perception can and ought to be separated from prior experiences, ideas, and associations and that the process of aesthetic significance and valuing occurs only when we attend to those qualities which are directly given in perception. In this way a separate domain—abstracted from the flow of more typical experiences and exchanges—is created for those activities and experiences which are described as "aesthetic."

The impersonal, abstract nature of this account of aesthetic experience must be seriously challenged. We must rigorously question the possibility and desirability of aesthetic participants dissociating their own thoughts, experiences, and impressions from their aesthetic encounters, leaving the object to control and dominate the exchange between object and perceiver. Again, while such injunctions may be regarded simply as reminders to concentrate on the object and not on extraneous recollections and musings, the depersonalization of our aesthetic exchanges needs to be carefully and critically examined.

It is a conceptual mistake to suppose that the aesthetic perception of formal qualities can be undertaken in an interpretive vacuum, that such perception is "merely" fixed, concentrated attention to such perceptible qualities as the work may possess in and of itself. We do not, and cannot, know the significance of objects, much less the symbols for objects (as in the case of representational art), without some active, essentially social process of acquiring this knowledge. The meanings we attach to objects, actions, and symbols are social in the sense that we must be familiar with, or have adopted consciously or otherwise, certain social traditions or conventions (ours and/or a particular society's or group's) in order for these to have significance for us. Two examples will illuminate this point.

A machine operator depicted with body bent and subdued, clothes dirtied, head bowed, and so on, may signal different things to art appreciators who have different knowledge bases with regard to the events that are represented. Suppose one percipient is aware that the person depicted was in fact a wage worker, caught in the midst of a revolutionary struggle, suffering from long-standing exploitation, abuse, discrimination, and so on. Further suppose that a second appreciator, unaware of these social and historical facts, sees the person pictured as a nineteenth-century artisan enjoying the toil involved in his labor of love. For these two respondents, the painting will have quite different meanings. Different kinds of experience will result depending on whether or not the appreciator possesses social and historical knowledge about this painting and the person depicted in it. Note that I am not suggesting here that one person's experience will be "aesthetic" while the other's will not. Rather, a level of understanding and appreciation is unavailable to the viewer who does not share this knowledge. Both presumably see the same pigments, lines, shapes, etc.—in short, the same formal, surface qualities—yet each person's aesthetic experience is affected by the kinds of knowledge brought to the actual experience of those surface qualities and by the interpretations that result. Each attaches a different meaning to the painting as a result.

Consider as a further example the song by Bob Dylan entitled "Hurricane." Given the guidelines of attitude theories of aesthetic experience, we ought to attend to the formal qualities and components of the medium itself, i.e., the elements of the song, including its rhythm, melody, word usage, pattern of rhyme, and the like. We ought to recognize the poetic form and imagery of the words, the musical elements that support the lyrics, and how these interact and reinforce each other; perhaps we would use such categories as balance, opposition, and the like in the process of analyzing this work of art. On this view, when we are able to listen to the song with these things in mind, to analyze how successfully these aesthetic elements work together, we may reasonably claim to have perceived and valued this song aesthetically. We will have paid attention to the formal or surface qualities of the work, perceived how these relate to one another, and so on. Such an analysis seems all that is required or aesthetically possible via the adoption of attitude theories that generate an aesthetic response.

Yet we cannot have an adequate understanding of the meaning of this song without some knowledge of the specific incident about which it was composed. Further, we cannot appreciate this artwork, at least on one level, without being aware of the history of racial injustices and oppression suffered by people of color, their struggles for social justice, equitable and fair treatment under the law, and so on. Words, whether in a song or in a conversation, have social meanings; so do pictorial and other kinds of symbol systems. These things do not have individual, unique meanings for particular people, meanings that can be read and understood in isolation from more encompassing events and social interactions. Prohibiting such a social context from informing our aesthetic experiences unduly restricts and impoverishes a work's aesthetic meaning and significance. While we may become sensitized to and appreciate the various relationships among the surface features of Dylan's "Hurricane" through the operation of a presentational aesthetic, we miss something centrally important about the value of this song if we restrict ourselves to such formal elements.

These examples show how prior knowledge and experiences are necessarily a part of our actual encounter with works of art and why the notion of dislocating our aesthetic experiences from other exchanges and events must be rejected as conceptually mistaken and, in a real sense, humanly impossible. Seeing bits of paint on canvas as representing a person, understanding the words of a song to refer to social realities—these are not things that can be accomplished by the insertion of psychical distance or by disallowing "external" social experience. We need a previous fund of experiences to draw on. Attaching meaning to lines, colors, shapes, words, and phrases, much less finding them significant for our lives, necessarily involves us as aesthetic participants in the process of applying socially derived knowledge to the perceptual field which composes the surface of aesthetic objects.

Nelson Goodman puts this point well with respect to pictorial representation in art. Goodman reminds us that "there is no innocent eye. The eye comes always ancient to its work, obsessed by its own past and by old and new insinuations of the ear, nose, tongue, fingers, heart, and brain. It functions not as an instrument self-powered and alone, but as a dutiful member of a complex and capricious organism. Not only how but what it sees is regulated by need and prejudice. It selects, rejects, organizes, discriminates, associates, classifies, analyzes, constructs. It does not so much mirror as take and make; and what it takes and makes it sees not bare, as items without attributes, but as things, as food, as people, as enemies, as stars, as weapons. Nothing is seen nakedly or naked."[7]

The crucial point here is that we do not passively receive isolatable sense impressions (whether visual, aural, or whatever) that are somehow the pure, correct raw data which we subsequently interpret and categorize, and to which we ascribe value. Perception and interpretation are inseparable such that whenever we perceive an object or event we also engage in interpretation—even when the interpretive act is more or less instantaneous, as when the object perceived is well known. The view that discerning and understanding an aesthetic object consists in interpreting and deciphering the sense data that we objectively have available is simply incorrect. The social nature of art and the aesthetic and the seamless nature of perception lead to inquiry about various conditions which give the object its full meaning, and hence its full significance.

Art objects are created at particular moments in history, within specific social contexts, and in light of extant traditions within and outside the domain of art. It is clear that the plays of Aeschylus and the writings of Homer were written within Greek traditions and frames of reference, just as it is clear that Dylan's "Hurricane" was composed within rather different traditions and social realities. Those realities help make artworks what they are—they would not be the same if they were written within other cultures and traditions. In general, the experiences of creative artists, and the social patterns and organizations inherent in the society in which they live, as well as the social institutions, cultural forms and patterns, traditions, and so on, that surround them, affect the nature and possibilities for artistic creation. While we must be careful to avoid the sort of determinism here which might discount or disallow the realization of truly creative, divergent, tradition-shattering art forms and works, and while cross-cultural, transhistorical understandings of a sort are possible and valuable, this should not obscure the ways in which the social milieu in which the artist is embedded helps shape the character and nature of the creative artist's endeavors,[8] and the ways that appreciators interpret them.

Just as the social context of the artist is something of which we need to be aware, so too are the social circumstances of the audience that interacts with the artwork. While the distinction between meaning and significance utilized earlier was useful for certain analytic purposes, we must also realize that aesthetic meanings do not reside in isolated, abstracted objects themselves, but are created out of an interaction between them and the intentional, personally engaged attention of individuals; in this sense aesthetic meaning and significance are interactive, both requiring an understanding of contexts other than those provided by the "bare work of art." Changing social circumstances may in fact alter the meaning of specific art objects for subsequent audiences. Meanings may be precluded, created, or altered with corresponding changes in artistic and social traditions. This is especially clear in the case of literature, where various words, phrases, and passages in an original text may entirely lose their meaning and be "misunderstood" by later audiences; or, new meanings may emerge and become attached to passages within the text, thus transforming the literary work so that subsequent audiences perceive virtually a new text when compared with the way it was understood originally. Just as we need to be aware of how the artist's circumstances affect his/her creative activities, then, we need also to keep in mind how the response of aesthetic participants may be tempered by their particular, contemporaneous experiences and perspectives.

These considerations argue against the sort of asocial, ahistorical characterization of aesthetic experience central to modern aesthetic theory. Rather than seeing aesthetic objects as autonomous, unconnected, disembodied entities to be viewed and valued in isolation from any important context, we need to recognize how both artistic creation and aesthetic appreciation are socially and historically bounded. The arguments presented above suggest that situating aesthetic forms within their social contexts must lie near the center of any adequate aesthetic theory.[9]

Still other factors become important in exposing the inadequacy of the notion that aesthetics demarcates a separate universe. The first section of this chapter suggested that the nature of aesthetic meaning and significance is inadequately dealt with by such an abstracted view of the aesthetic. The reality of a social and historical character for creating and appreciating art is, as well, masked by such a view. Yet more needs to be said about the impersonal, disembodied nature of aesthetic perception and appreciation within the modern tradition. Seeing how aesthetic response is the result of an interactive process, necessarily involving a particular object and an actively involved participant—in short how aesthetic response is a dialectical process—will lead to new ways of thinking about aesthetic value.

In arguing for the relevance of aesthetic considerations in all experience, Donald Arnstine examines a painting by Charles Burchfield, *Black Houses*.[10] Arnstine distinguishes between the form of the painting and what he calls its "sign-content."[11] He makes two points about a work's sign-content that are especially relevant. First, whenever we attend to a work of art we always see the formal elements and its sign-content as conjoined; only analytically can we distinguish between the two. The meaning of an aesthetic object is derived not from its form or content in isolation, but out of the interaction which exists between these two elements of aesthetic objects: a change in one necessitates or entails a change in the other. Thus, when analyzing a work of art, we must be careful about cataloguing only the formal elements of the work, as if these are separable from what the work expresses.

Second, Arnstine points out that any object or artifact, not just a work of art, is capable of having form or of being perceived as containing an aesthetically interesting form. Yet natural events are not planned by any human being and so cannot be said to be designed or created with certain formal features in mind. The pattern of thunder on a stormy night or the melodic sounds of a woodland stream tumbling its way through a forest cannot be said to be the intentional result of a human creator. But we do in fact sometimes find the sounds of thunder or a stream to be aesthetically enjoyable, in part, because of the formal qualities of these events. It would seem, then, that an object which has an aesthetically interesting form is not dependent upon an artificer to produce it in some purposive way.

The obvious rejoinder here is that if we do not see form *in* the object or event because it has been put there by a creator, then it must be somehow caused by actions on the part of the perceiver. That is, form, as has been alleged in the case of both beauty and pornography, must be in the eye of the beholder, not in the object itself. Yet surely this is too hasty a judgment: claiming to have perceived aesthetically interesting form in something is not justified merely by so stating. We would not, for example, easily accept the view that the seemingly endless string of fast-food establishments found in most cities in this country has an aesthetically interesting form, regardless of the intensity of one's sentiments in this regard. We might, on the other hand, accept this judgment if it were pointed out how some of the elements in the visual field were related in a formally interesting way. Perhaps the combination of shapes, colors, lines, etc., in the scene might be construed as aesthetically significant when viewed from a particular angle or at a specific time of day.

The upshot of this view is that, although neither intentional activity by an artist nor the activities and beliefs of some perceiver are by themselves responsible for our aesthetic reaction to a certain object or artifact, such a reaction "is a function of our perception of objects and events, not of the objects themselves. People do not of course, create form out of their heads. For perception itself is a function of a total event in which a person and some part of his environment participate."[12] The perception of form in objects, in other words, is part of a dialectical interaction of the object with a participant. Form resides in neither of these independently. The usual distinction between objectivity and subjectivity is less than helpful in this context, since aesthetic experience necessarily blends these perspectives. These considerations raise serious questions about the viability of any notion of aesthetic response which displaces or makes problematic the active role of an aesthetic participant in the construction of aesthetic meaning and value.[13]

The importance of an actively involved participant is, of course, as true of our interactions with artworks as it is of interactions with natural events. Form, even that which seems obviously a part of a work of art, is not in the work. As Arnstine points out with respect to the previously mentioned example, "Mr. Burchfield did not put form in his painting [of *Black Houses*]; he put paint on a plane surface."[14] To see these bits of paint as representing houses requires personal, active involvement and knowledge of a certain sort, knowledge which is itself socially and historically bounded. It is out of this interplay of an informed, responsive, active participant with the form and content of an object or event that aesthetic experience arises.

In addition to aesthetic meanings relying on socially and historically contextualized knowledge, Arnstine further elucidates how aesthetic experience has a more personal, psychologically oriented aspect or phase. First of all, it should be noted that not all perception is concerned with appreciation of an object's form: we do not normally read a piece of philosophical discourse, for example, with a view to its formal, symbolic organization. What is missing from such perception, says Arnstine, is affective arousal—we are just not interested in, or excited by, the visual properties of the text. When our interest in considering a piece of philosophical writing is familiar and habitual, its visual qualities normally go unnoticed and arouse in us little affect. And our way of looking at such texts, disregarding their possible aesthetic import, is guided by the realization that our attention to the text's visual/aesthetic qualities is usually not repaid with any significant degree of aesthetic satisfaction. But when we view something that is perhaps less familiar, say the text of certain children's books or some poetry, the perception of the formal qualities may arouse our interest; for example, the way words are arranged on the page, the manner in which paragraphs are laid out, etc., may be visually interesting. At the same time that such interest is aroused, the piece becomes affective (as well as effective) and valued. In other words, "neither perception, meaning, nor affect can occur in isolation; they are but different aspects of the same event, of a single psychological process."[15] Meaning, in short, can be separated neither from affective response nor from an individual's perception and purposes. The example Arnstine offers of a driver trainee and a more experienced driver illustrates how the same object perceived by both—an approaching twenty-thousand-pound semitrailer, for instance-will arouse different levels or kinds of affect and will have as a result different kinds of significance.

Two points about Arnstine's explication of aesthetic meaning deserve emphasis. First, although form and content are inseparable in actual aesthetic experience, the observation of a piece of art as having a certain form and embodying a specific content is a relational process involving (1) an interaction between form and content and (2) an object and a perceiver. Better, we might say that the dichotomization within each of these two categories is artificial, hindering our understanding of art and its significance. Aesthetic meaning does not reside in a phenomenologically objective field accessible only to rarefied aesthetic perception, but exists in the dialectical interaction between surface and interpretation, subject and object. Second, the significance and value of an object is in part related to the interests we have in it. For example, even so common an event as the ringing of a telephone will have a different significance if we are waiting anxiously for a reply from a close friend returning after a long absence. A different level of affective arousal will result inasmuch as the ringing which eventually occurs will evoke intense sensory qualities and generate a qualitatively different experience.

Conclusions

The arguments and considerations presented in this chapter expose the weaknesses and insufficiencies embedded in the philosophical underpinnings of the tenets included in modern aesthetic theory. Taken together, these arguments show in what respects this tradition is less than credible as a basis for understanding the fullness and richness that constitute the aesthetic domain. The autonomy of the aesthetic first proposed by

Baumgarten, the refinements or extensions of this position postulated by subsequent thinkers such as Kant, and the more contemporary appeals by Bullough, Ingarden, and Stolnitz serve to promote a separate universe for the aesthetic within which our participation with objects may be regarded as genuinely aesthetic. Within this universe, aesthetic experience is asocial and ahistorical, an experience in which we perceive and value objects intrinsically.

This view of aesthetics is of more than scholarly interest. On the one hand, as we have seen, the philosophical positions constructed by advocates of modern theories of the aesthetic experience were created to ensure that artistic creations of certain kinds would be valued and also governed by a particular kind of absorption. It does seem to be the case that this perspective was useful for highlighting the "fine," "high," or "elite" arts. Creating such a lofty and removed ideal for aesthetic perception, and providing in the process a kind of ontological status for art that might be reverential, also led to a distinction between "intrinsic/inherent" values and "extrinsic/derivative" values related to forms of human expression. There is reason to think that the generation of a particular form of aesthetic attitude and perception, removed from everyday life, helped generate the distinction between "the fine arts" and "the popular arts," and especially between "art" and "popular culture."

On the other hand, some of the ideas contained in modern aesthetic theories have been echoed in programmatic initiatives in education. Perhaps the best contemporary example of this is contained in the conceptual portion of the program in aesthetic education developed through the Central Midwestern Regional Education Laboratory (CEMREL).[16] The philosophical foundation for this program conceived of aesthetic experience as pertaining to the immediate appearance of objects and as being phenomenological, in the sense that this appearance is separated from other experiences and perceptions; intrinsically valuable; disconnected from personal actions outside the experience itself; and fundamentally amoral, apolitical, and non-ideological.

In the curriculum packages and resulting experiences created for elementary school students in the CEMREL program, aesthetic experiences are self-contained and separated from the day-to-day experiences, interests, and concerns of children. Aesthetic experience is seen, as a result, as artificial and, in a sense, unreal. Little is discussed in the curriculum unit entitled "Relating Sound and Movement," for example, about the linkages between aesthetic forms and broader interests, commitments, and concerns. One of the things learned by students, hence, is that though the aesthetic may serve a decorative function, it has little to do with the way people think and act in other life situations. Given the emphasis on students' understanding "continuums within pitch, tempo and amount of intensity in sound; within amount of space, amount of time, and amount of force in movement,"[17] we can see how a Formalist approach serves to dislocate the aesthetic from other domains, personal and social. By focusing on particular qualities in sound and movement activities and by comparing and contrasting various kinds of emphases, the students develop certain skills of discrimination (with the typical pre- and posttest measures of competence). A deeper understanding of sounds and movements, or the value and significance of those elements, gives way to an emphasis on a sequenced, highly regularized curriculum form tied to an abstracted, formalized aesthetic. If the arguments presented in this chapter serve as a counter to the tradition of aesthetic attitude theories, they oppose the conceptual underpinnings of CEMREL's Aesthetic Education Program as well. A beginning effort in the development of a different kind of aesthetic education program might be to provide appreciative activities linked to students' and their families' lives, perhaps followed by creative efforts at analyzing and creating artifacts of personal, familial, and social meaning. That kind of programmatic initiative might well involve students in forms of popular culture.

The view that attending to the immediate appearance of objects—their formal, sensual surfaces—can be clearly understood or have intense meaning for children or adults, or can have significance in isolation from past experiences and perceptions, must be rejected. Even aesthetic form, to be recognized as such, must be placed in a context wherein the colors, shapes, and lines of an object are understood as signifying or representing something other than themselves. Interpreting and deciphering pigments on canvas or ink marks on paper require us apply the accumulated knowledge that we possess to these immediate perceptions. Any theory of art and aesthetic experience that separates such immediate perceptions from previous, or future, knowledge and understanding, or that disallows art from having meaning outside our direct experience with it, must be rejected as a basis for explaining the value of aesthetic experience.

It follows from this that our interaction with aesthetic objects cannot in any strict sense be phenomenological. To the extent that "phenomenological objectivity" involves viewing an object apart from our own dispositions, inclinations, and affections, it must be regarded as an empty aesthetic doctrine or article of faith rather than as an adequate description or prescription for what aesthetic experience is or should be. To perceive an art object or aesthetic experience phenomenologically (if this is possible), is to see it in a way that diminishes its meaning. We cannot separate an object's meaning and significance from our perception of and responses to it, the latter of which get mediated, necessarily, by our own personal and individual dispositions as well as by the social and historical influences which surround and help create these dispositions.

What then is to be made of the concept of intrinsic value? Intrinsic value is only possible if we attend to the object with lenses that are asocial, ahistorical, phenomenological, and disconnected. Since this kind of perception is, as we have seen, itself problematic, so too is the notion of intrinsic worth in aesthetic experience. Aesthetic objects can be understood and have value for participants only when they are placed within the context of the participants' other experiences, associations, and activities.

Lastly, the aesthetic experience inextricably contains a social element. In both their creative and appreciative aspects, artworks and the aesthetic are social phenomena, always constructed and understood within the context of some fund of acquired knowledge, understanding, and interpretation. Apart from this context, the meaning of aesthetic experience is diminished and its significance is all but eliminated.

Thus, the picture of the aesthetic articulated in chapter 1 must be rejected as conceptually inadequate. The concerns presented here show that a sophisticated theory of aesthetic response must include considerations of the aesthetic object's historical and social context, the dispositions and propensities of the viewer, and the work's connection with the larger topic of human interests and concerns generally. How meaning is derived from the interaction between subject and object and how aesthetic significance and value are connected with activities outside the aesthetic situation itself must also be addressed. Aesthetic experience cannot fully develop in a separate universe.

Even though many of the components of modern aesthetic theory are inadequate philosophically, this group of postulates and perspectives may serve other than theoretical interests. In particular, we need to question the ideological constructs that may be furthered, buffered, or augmented within society by the theoretical positions that underlie certain presuppositions and assumptions. In other words, philosophical and educational debate involves more than just rational discussion over theoretical issues. It serves other interests as well.[18] Understanding the ideological role of aesthetic theory and of curriculum materials will occupy the next chapter, as we will take up the question of how schools serve as agents of economic and cultural reproduction.

Notes

1. See, for example, George Dickie, "All Aesthetic Attitude Theories Fail: The Myth of the Aesthetic Attitude," in *Aesthetics: A Critical Anthology*, ed. George Dickie and Richard J. Sclafani (New York: St. Martin's Press, 1977); Marshall Cohen, "Aesthetic Essence," in *Philosophy in America*, ed. Max Black (Ithaca: Cornell University Press, 1965); and George Dickie, "Psychical Distance: In a Fog at Sea," *British Journal of Aesthetics* 13, no. 1 (Winter 1973).

2. One of the central questions involved here, of course, is what constitutes the proper or legitimate domain of aesthetic experience—and thus can be construed as legitimate aesthetic value.

3. As we shall see more clearly later, in the second part of this chapter, the distinction between meaning and significance is only useful for analytic purposes; indeed, they share some important similarities. Yet at this preliminary step in our analysis, this distinction will prove helpful.

4. See DeWitt H. Parker, *The Principles of Aesthetics* (Boston: Silver, Burdett, and Co., 1920), and Stephen C. Pepper, *Principles of Art Appreciation* (New York: Harcourt, Brace, & World, 1949).

5. Consider, for instance, the ability to discriminate between "red" and "green" stoplights at an intersection.

6. Landon E. Beyer, "Aesthetic Curriculum and Cultural Reproduction," in *Ideology and Practice in Schooling*, ed. Michael W. Apple and Lois Weis (Philadelphia: Temple University Press, 1983).

7. Nelson Goodman, *Languages of Art* (Indianapolis: Bobbs Merrill Company, 1968), pp. 7–8.

8. See, for example, Carol Duncan and Alan Wallach, "The Museum of Modern Art as Late Capitalist Ritual: An Iconographic Analysis," *Marxist Perspectives* 1, no. 4 (Winter 1978); and Walter Benjamin, "The Work of Art in the Age of Mechanical Reproduction," in his *Illuminations,* ed. Hannah Arendt (New York: Schocken Books, 1969).

9. See in this context John Berger, *Ways of Seeing* (New York: Penguin Books, 1977).

10. Donald Arnstine, *Philosophy of Education: Learning and Schooling* (New York: Harper & Row, 1967).

11. Ibid., p. 178.

12. Arnstine, *Philosophy of Education*, p. 183.

13. See in this context David Bleich, *Subjective Criticism* (Baltimore: The Johns Hopkins University Press, 1978).

14. Arnstine, *Philosophy of Education*, p. 183.

15. Ibid., p. 190.

16. Histories of this effort to create an aesthetic education curriculum can be found in CEMREL, *The CEMREL Aesthetic Education Program: A Report on the Accomplishments, 1969–1975, vol. 1* (St. Louis: CEMREL, 1976); and Manuel Barkan, Laura Chapman, and Evan Kern, *Guidelines: Curriculum Development for Aesthetic Education* (St. Louis: CEMREL, 1970).

17. CEMREL, CEMREL Program, "Relating Sound and Movement" unit, "Teacher's Guide," p. 6.

18. See Landon E. Beyer, *Knowing and Acting: Inquiry, Ideology, and Educational Studies* (London: Falmer Press, 1988).

Chapter 3

Education and Cultural Reproduction

The previous chapter explored the deficiencies inherent in a "presentational aesthetic" and in so doing assisted us in seeing how the historical and social contexts within which aesthetic responses take place are important for understanding their meaning. The isolation of art and aesthetic experience, their dislocation from everyday life and cultural patterns, serves to undermine the value of aesthetic activities. Those tendencies became central to modern aesthetic theory and are embedded in the philosophical orientation that provided the conceptual grounding for the aesthetic education curriculum materials in the CEMREL program.

This chapter focuses on the ways in which curriculum content and form, and the kinds of practices that are generated via the school curriculum, often serve larger political and ideological interests. A critical framework is provided for understanding and assessing the theoretical assumptions and practical actions that take place in schools and their relation to dominant social, economic, and cultural patterns. The analyses presented undermine the view that typical school practices are benign or neutral, or unrelated to larger social dynamics. We cannot understand why schools and classrooms operate as they do—what kinds of knowledge are valued, which groups of students are provided access to what perspectives and interpretations, what measures are used to evaluate individual students and classroom practices—if we see them as isolated from larger social realities.

A central normative question that is related to the possibility of contextualizing school practices is how we construe the "unit of analysis" when we evaluate students, teachers, and programs, as well as new ideas and possibilities.[1] That is, how do we determine what we are to look for and at when undertaking some kind of evaluation? How we frame and formulate this unit of analysis is usually not the result of conscious, rational deliberation and debate; rather, it is strongly influenced by the very assumptions or presuppositions that are tacitly held by teachers, administrators, and the public. As Erik Olin Wright has noted, the very questions that we ask "are always embedded in conceptual structures and if these structures lack certain pivotal elements . . . certain questions cannot or will not be asked."[2] Thus the very theoretical suppositions that educators hold often specify what kinds of questions will be asked and what the proper unit of analysis for their resolution should be. Throughout this chapter, fundamental, seemingly obvious questions will be asked, questions such as what is curriculum, what kinds of things are schools, what do they do, whose interests do they further, and so on, so that we might consider the parameters of those suppositions, the interests that they serve, and what a new unit of analysis might require.[3]

It is not uncommon for evaluative processes to be guided by the assumption that schools and curriculum are relatively isolated, independent phenomena with little if any important connection with other institutional patterns and social realities. As elaborated below, the tendency in education has been to conceive of the development and evaluation of curricula as standardized, achievement-centered, ideologically neutral phenomena that are immersed within a set of benign, meritocratic institutional processes and arrangements; within this framework schools become seen as asocial and politically neutral.

Such a disconnected approach to understanding curriculum and teaching is inadequate and conceptually shortsighted. An understanding of the social role of schooling and curriculum has been furthered by contemporary scholarship in the sociology of school knowledge, scholarship that illuminates what schools actually seem to do, "under the surface" or "naturally." By looking at how critical traditions in curriculum inquiry have helped us better understand how schools are part of a complex, sometimes reciprocally reinforcing network of ideological apparatuses—principally in their role as agents of economic and cultural reproduction—we will see what is at issue within this growing body of writing. This discussion will also outline how other ways of thinking about curriculum matters can lead to informative analyses and how those ways of thinking can be brought to bear on questions of curriculum development and evaluation. By looking at attempts to situate schools within a political, social, and economic context, we will see how curriculum is often tied, albeit unintentionally for the most part, to the maintenance of current institutional arrangements, and how our unit of analysis must be broadened to include such contextual elements. It is precisely these connections, between the school curriculum and the larger society, which then become our unit of analysis. A more socially sensitive analysis of schools, curricula, and teaching practices will be illuminating for an understanding of the ways in which curriculum programs and practices function within our educational system.[4]

Reproduction in Education

Education is at once a process that has apparently been a part of all societies and cultures; a field of inquiry with particular traditions, literatures, and perspectives that change over time; and the name of a particular range of institutions. When we inquire into the fundamental aims and purposes of education, we are met with a host of possibilities: for instance, to provide entrance to specific occupations and careers, to promote new ways of thinking, or to gain access to some elevated status or position. More generally, we might say, with Dewey, that education is responsible for the generation of "social continuity,"[5] or the sustaining of ways of life over time. This process might include the inculcation of beliefs, practices, forms of knowledge, ways of thinking, values, and attitudes.

While education does play a central role in social continuity, though, it also has a critical role in terms of which beliefs, practices, etc., should be continued and which should not. The development of an educational agenda must be involved in forging critically important directions about what kinds of beliefs and practices are worth saving or should be discarded, what kinds of values are important for generating a particular kind of society, what moral qualities are linked to social life, and so on. In other words, those committed to education must be prepared not only to blindly continue current social patterns, but to develop alternative ideas and practices that generate more valuable forms of personal interaction and social justice.

Yet it is abundantly clear that not all educators take that more elaborated, critical view of the purposes of education. In an important essay dealing with recurring issues and themes in curriculum, Herbert M. Kliebard argues that the field as a whole is "characterized by an overwhelmingly ameliorative orientation."[6] Such an ameliorative stance may be in part created by "the huge constituency of teachers, school administrators, and supervisors who exert continual pressure on those who conduct research for answers to such practical questions as, how can I improve my teaching, which are the best programs, and how can I recognize and reward a good teacher."[7] Teachers, in turn, are themselves continually confronted with practical questions from students and others, questions which often require immediate responses. Frequently the demand for some kind of response or intervention on the part of teachers makes it impossible for them to engage in a sustained, reflective analysis of the immediate situation; more, the nature and pace of classroom life almost always prevents the possibility of teachers engaging with colleagues in inquiry and discussions related to educational literatures and issues. In a larger sense, one consequence of the pace of classroom activities and the depth and type of discourse that is possible in them is that schooling "revolves around the effort to develop a kind of technology of teaching leading to the performance of certain presumably effective behaviors in the absence of any fundamental understanding or conception of what kind of activity teaching is."[8] It is very easy to conceive of and confront teaching, within the pragmatic orientation that exists in many schools, as a technical enterprise, with success and failure measured in rather technical and quantifiable terms (e.g., as exhibited by scores on achievement tests or instruments used to identify "exceptional children," ratings on supervisory evaluation forms, and so on). Another consequence of this pragmatic, technological orientation to teaching is an overemphasis on teaching technique and method, abstracted from any principled, deep understanding of the educational ideas and ideals which stand behind and give such methods meaning.[9]

The field of curriculum itself has been guided and informed, if not actually dominated, by such technical concerns. A substantial number of educators seem to limit their investigations into the nature and effects of schooling—into what counts as effective school practice—to two broad areas: those dealing with measures of (usually individual) academic proficiency, on the one hand, and socialization effectiveness, on the other. Though in many instances these two areas have been collapsed into a single pedagogical perspective, the traditions of academic achievement and socialization still form a good deal of the conceptual apparatus underlying the "common sense" of what schools are about.[10] Each of these traditions, in addition to being directed and dominated by technical concerns, views the function or purpose of educational institutions as socially and politically neutral. In effect, technical concerns have served to defuse and displace more fundamental political and ethical debate within educational discourse.[11]

One of the most well known analyses of the allegedly neutral socialization effects of schools can be found in Robert Dreeben's book, *On What*

Is Learned in School.[12] Much of Dreeben's explication of what has come to be called the "hidden curriculum" of schools is concerned with how family life and school life each make a contribution to larger social experience.[13] The structural/functional view of socialization embraced by Dreeben moves him to acknowledge what he labels an "ideological caveat": he explains to the reader that "the main purpose of this analysis is to present a formulation, hypothetical in nature, of how schooling contributes to the emergence of certain psychological outcomes, and not to provide an apology or justification for those outcomes on ideological grounds."[14] In addition to not providing the reader with any such ideological justification, Dreeben also fails to examine the possible ideological functions of the "psychological outcomes" he considers. It is this tendency to construct a non-ideological, apolitical analysis of the socialization effects of schooling that continues to be influential in thinking about educational practice. Socialization thus becomes a technical concern to discover the "best way" or "most effective method" to promote the adoption of the correct or appropriate social norms in students; infused with such a technical rubric, these norms are, correlatively, conceived of as "given" rather than as socially constructed and to that extent problematic, open to critique, and changeable.[15]

Within the achievement model, likewise, curricular knowledge has often been thought of as unproblematic, even as teachers and teacher educators search for "best practices" to enhance student accomplishments. The school curriculum may be implemented by teachers out of a "common sense" idea of "what knowledge is of most worth," preselected by "authorities" outside the classroom (e.g., textbook adoption committees or district administrators), or, now perhaps, encouraged because of its ability to lead us into the new millennium. Epistemological and ideological questions such as what is the nature of curricular knowledge, how is the selection process which produces "school knowledge" itself governed, whose knowledge gets into schools (and whose doesn't), what is to count as an instance of having learned something, and the like, are often not carefully considered; in their place, concerns about how best to structure, implement, package, sequence, and evaluate those forms of knowledge which find their way into classrooms become central matters for educational investigation. Thus the achievement tradition becomes more and more given over to bureaucratic concerns for control, efficiency, and certainty, leaving the formal corpus of school knowledge largely unexamined.

Both the achievement and socialization traditions may be viewed as important aspects of the functionalist perspective in curriculum and as responding to the ameliorative and technological concerns of school people as outlined by Kliebard; each treats its respective body of content or organizational form as authoritatively pre-given, usually from "outside" or "above." The possible latent functions of the selection processes themselves, and of schooling in general, go unrecognized and unnoticed, thereby confirming and legitimating the perception of schools as politically and ideologically neutral. When immediate, predominantly technical concerns dominate the thinking of educators, the less than immediately obvious effects of schooling become at best secondary, and the school's status as politically neutral is confirmed. Floud and Halsey point out the social consequences of such a position: "The structural functionalist is preoccupied with social integration based on shared values—that is with consensus—and he conducts his analysis solely in terms of the motivational actions of individuals. For him, therefore, education is a means motivating individuals to behave in ways appropriate to maintain society in a state of equilibrium."[16]

This assumption of neutrality, social stability, and cultural continuity on the part of educational theorists and practitioners has come under increasing scrutiny and has been called into question from several quarters. Among others, this assumption has been seriously questioned by the sociology of education, and specifically by theorists of economic and cultural reproduction.[17] This has led to extensive debates and discussions regarding the precise nature of the relationship between classroom activities and the larger social order. By examining the outlines of these discussions we will be in a better position to see how the evaluation process in curriculum must be expanded to investigate such ideological concerns and perspectives.

Schooling as Economic Reproduction

In the contemporary era, it was the publication of *Schooling in Capitalist America* that situated the school as one of a number of important institutions which together help perpetuate the current social order.[18] Bowles and Gintis view the function of schooling as a fundamentally economic one, responding to the needs of a particular form of economic organization. This position is forcefully advanced, in fact, in the authors' view of socialization: "Our critique of education and other aspects of human development in the United States fully recognizes the necessity of some form of socialization. The critical question is: What for? In the United States the human development experience is dominated by an undemocratic, irrational, and exploitative economic structure. Young people have no recourse from the requirements of the system but a life of poverty, dependence, and economic insecurity."[19] Schools serve to produce a "finished product" that will have sufficiently mastered the requisite skills and dispositions to ensure the continuation of workers for American corporate capitalism; educational institutions function in a way that guarantees the reproduction of a particular economic form. There are, on the authors' view, four main components to this relationship between educational and economic structure. These include (1) an adequate and appropriately trained labor supply provided by the educational establishment; (2) social relationships within schools which can be used to "facilitate the translation of labor power into profits";[20] (3) a system of acknowledging, rewarding, and reinforcing personality traits that are shared by the school and the economic spheres; and (4) a stratified and hierarchical way of thinking about one's relationship with others, a way that is developed in schools through a differential system of status and distinctions and which has utility in the marketplace.

Bowles and Gintis argue that the social relationships within schools correspond to the division of labor, along hierarchical lines, within the economic order. In schools, vertical lines of authority and power exist and become part of everyday classroom experience, with students at the low end of the power continuum, followed by teachers and administrators. This pattern of domination is in turn duplicated in many workplaces: individual workers stand on the bottom rung of the authority ladder while the foreman or supervisor oversees their work, with the manager/owner providing direction and incentives (positive and negative). Just as this pattern of social relations in the sphere of economic production creates alienated labor, and an alienated workforce, so too is the student alienated from his or her own educational experience.

Bowles and Gintis further argue that schools function to prepare particular social groups for specific occupational slots while reserving different occupations for other groups. Not only are alternative curricula devised, for example, for vocationally oriented and college-bound high school students, but different behavioral norms are enacted and enforced as well. And as differently oriented classrooms develop their own sets of dispositional rules, social relations of widely varying sorts are facilitated. It is in the correspondence between these social relations within each curricular track and the norms mandated by particular occupational slots that, the authors allege, the potency of our economic system for school settings may be seen. "Thus in high school, vocational and general tracks emphasize rule-following and close supervision, while the college track tends toward a more open atmosphere emphasizing the internalization of norms."[21]

In contrast to the achievement and socialization traditions, theorists of economic reproduction view the activities of schools as intimately tied to the demands of a hierarchical, alienating economic system. School experiences further the interests of certain groups and classes while effectively curtailing those of others. Indeed, in arguing for a correspondence between schooling and economic form, it seems that Bowles and Gintis are attempting to expose the perniciousness of the former by virtue of its complicity with the latter.

As a number of authors have argued, there are several ways in which such an analysis is at least misleading. What Bowles and Gintis provide, though in many ways insightful, is often little more than a "black box" view of schooling, with particular inputs and outputs; what happens inside this black box, the actual classroom exchanges and forms of knowledge which may in some way solidify social and economic forms, is for the most part neglected.[22] This is more than just an academic or scholarly issue, especially for those interested in how the activities of teachers, administrators, and others may concretely serve ideological interests, and for those interested in understanding how educational activities might be redirected so as to serve other interests.

The relationship between schooling and economic form is also described by Bowles and Gintis somewhat mechanistically, in at least two ways. Though the interfaces between schools and a capitalist economy make any notion of neutrality seem naive, it is not necessarily the case that there exists a simple one-to-one correspondence between schooling and economic production. Many students "caught" in the alienating and repressive classroom situations that Bowles and Gintis describe are by no means passive; they are frequently quite adept at exposing, seeing through, and struggling against the bureaucratic realities of school life that the authors describe.

Opposition to dominant messages and influences in the workplace is also a reality. As Richard Edwards, for example, has documented, "Hierarchy has changed as well as persisted, and in searching for what has caused this transformation I have come to realize that the primary catalyst for change is the continuing contention of classes, the struggle of capitalists, workers, and others to protect and advance their interests."[23]

Perhaps most important for the purposes of this chapter, theorists of economic reproduction may focus too narrowly on the economic sphere. Supposing that schools, teachers, and students simply respond passively to the demands of a relatively isolated, monolithic form of economic production is too reductionist a perspective. The social and ideological possibilities of educational institutions are not fully revealed by focusing on the ways in which some educators blindly comply with narrow economic initiatives.[24] Indeed, some teachers and administrators actively work to thwart those perspectives. This is not to deny the connections between schools and economic production. Rather, to expose the complex ideological functions of schooling and make them a subject for analysis, we need to (1) go beyond "merely" their relation to economic form, without losing sight of this vital aspect of social reproduction, and (2) recognize the active roles that committed, progressive teachers continue to play in classrooms.[25]

Schooling as Cultural Reproduction

One other problem with the view that schools only function as agents of economic reproduction is that it overlooks the domain of curriculum content itself. How school knowledge is related to ideological, social, and political purposes is not systematically addressed. It is just this relationship between the selection and organization of curricula and the power relations extant in society that Michael F. D. Young has explored in incisive ways.[26]

In discussing the state of the art of American sociology of education, Young suggests that a predominantly functionalist viewpoint "presupposes at a very general level an agreed upon set of societal values or goals which define both the selection and organization of knowledge in curricula."[27]

Young argues that "those in positions of power will attempt to define what is to be taken as knowledge, how accessible to different groups any knowledge is, and what are the accepted relationships between different knowledge areas and between those who have access to them and make them available."[28] With all the discussion of what has been termed the "knowledge explosion" during this century, and now especially the "technology revolution," it is all too easy to forget that knowledge forms in schools are not uniformly available to all social groups or classes, and that certain "technological advances" have enhanced the commodification of knowledge in universities, as those institutions further corporate structures and interests.[29]

What Young and others are suggesting is that schools "process" knowledge, in addition to "processing" people in the way that Bowles and Gintis document. Both processes in turn need to be linked with the unequal distribution of resources in advanced capitalist economies. How knowledge is selected and organized, in addition to how dispositional elements of classroom practice affect students' consciousness of themselves and others, therefore becomes important for understanding the ideological role of schools in maintaining and legitimating the current set of dominant institutional patterns and arrangements. Perhaps an example here will clarify the relationship between curriculum content and economic and political power.

In considering why technical expertise has come to be considered what he calls "high status knowledge," Michael W. Apple argues that, "a corporate economy requires the production of high levels of technical knowledge to keep the economic apparatus running effectively and to become more sophisticated in the maximization of opportunities for economic expansion . . . production of a particular 'commodity'. . . is of more concern than the distribution of that particular commodity. To the extent that it does not interfere with the production of technical knowledge, then concerns about distributing it more equitably can be tolerated as well."[30] The reason for this emphasis on the production of technical knowledge in, for example, the fields of medicine or engineering is that industry within a capitalist economy requires not an equitable distribution of such knowledge, but rather its increased production, to ensure its continual economic solvency; this in turn necessitates the increasingly specialized training of a relative few technological experts who can further expand the requisite high-status knowledge forms. Significantly, as a result, "cultural institutions 'naturally' generate levels of poor achievement."[31] An unequal and stratified social order, in short, depends more upon the stratification and perceived scarcity of those knowledge forms found valuable than upon ethical argumentation over the distribution of knowledge within educational institutions.

Like Young and Apple, Basil Bernstein views school knowledge as crucial in informing the quality of school experience and its relationship to social control within the wider society. Bernstein's analysis centers on those social and historical changes, especially those associated with the demands of an increasingly specialized division of labor, which have helped change the format for curricular offerings and pedagogical relationships.[32] He suggests that, beyond the time spent on particular subjects, there may be a more important perspective from which to view the curriculum. He develops this perspective by articulating the categories of classification and framing, as they can be applied to curricular and pedagogical relationships within schools. By "classification," Bernstein means the relative insulation or isolation of subject matter within the school's curriculum. Classification "refers to the nature of the differentiation between contents."[33] Strong classification schemes, where subject matter is increasingly important and authoritative, produce a sharply divided, compartmentalized curriculum. Weak classification schemes denote a blurring or weakening of curricular boundaries, as for example in many preschools and progressive classrooms. In such classrooms subject matter will be more interdependent and commingled, perhaps even to the point of being seamless. Thus, on Bernstein's view, "classification focuses our attention upon boundary strength as the critical distinguishing feature of the division of labor of educational knowledge. It gives us . . . the basic structure of the message system, curriculum."[34]

Framing, on the other hand, refers to the pedagogical relationships in the classroom and the relative amount of control, by teacher and student, over what is studied. Framing refers to the relative freedom of school people to organize, select, and pace the subjects of instruction. Educational frames, like classification schemes, can be either weak or strong, "weak" framing indicating a substantial amount of control over the selection, pacing, and timing of the curriculum, "strong" framing indicating little control in such matters.

Bernstein uses the notions of classification and framing to generate two types of educational "codes." He identifies integrated codes as those wherein subject matter boundaries are blurred and insulation is reduced; whereas collection codes are typified by strong boundaries between identifiable subject areas. The adoption of either educational code will have effects that go beyond the realm of curriculum. Differing pedagogical and evaluation forms will be embraced under each type of code and will affect the personal identities of teachers and students, the power relations within classrooms, and the concept of personal property. Moreover, "principles of power and social control are realized through educational knowledge codes and, through the codes, enter into and shape consciousness."[35]

Under collection codes the subject matter is the source of personal identification for both students and teachers. Within such classrooms, both teacher and student will tend to identify with their particular subject matter specialization. This will have an impact not only upon their sense of academic affiliation, but also upon the social relations within any given classroom. As Bernstein put this point, "It is the subject which becomes the lynch-pin of the identity. Any attempt to weaken or *change* classification strength (or even frame strength) may be felt as a threat to one's identity and may be experienced as a pollution endangering the sacred."[36]

When collection codes are dominant, the teacher is seen as authoritative, insofar as he or she "possesses" knowledge that the group desires. Since teachers are viewed as people who embody disciplinary knowledge, a special status is conferred upon them, a status which has a decided effect upon the dynamics of power within that group. Students are seen, and see themselves, as relatively powerless just because they do not possess what the teacher dispenses, namely, knowledge of that subject matter. Under integrated codes, however, the authority of the subject matter, and of the teacher in his/her embodiment of it, is replaced by some more general organizing principle which subsumes subject matter specialization under it.

The concept of "property" is similarly modified by the adoption of either educational code. Within integrated codes, it is not the possession of some particular kind of knowledge that is sought, but rather some more general, typically dispositional, quality—perhaps cooperativeness, psychological or therapeutic adjustment, individual initiative, and so on. On the other hand, "knowledge under collection [codes] is private property with its own power structure and market situation. Children and pupils are early socialized into this concept of knowledge as private property. They are encouraged to work as isolated individuals with their arms around their work."[37]

Bernstein argues that there has been, within the educational establishment, a shift from collected to integrated codes. There is decreasing emphasis, especially at the elementary school level, on the acquisition of subject matter, with a corresponding increase in the integration of curricular forms under some more general principle of organization. It is this shift that Bernstein suggests is reflective of changes in the division of labor in the wider society.

For Bernstein, changes in curriculum form, from collected to integrated codes, reflect and help support broader changes in society, from mechanical to organic solidarity, as the demands of an industrialized economy necessitate divergent forms of socialization and control. As the conception of private property and the relations of power which attend it accompany an evolving sense of labor specialization, it is important that the "messages" communicated through the organized symbolic system of the school—its curriculum—coincide with these broader social and economic transformations. By making subject matter less authoritative, and hence curriculum less insulated, those perceptions of property and power within the larger society are reinforced by the pedagogical practices and evaluation forms within the school.

The work of Young and Bernstein, as well as that of Bowles and Gintis, to a large extent leaves out of consideration how the activities of both students and teachers fit within their framework and, importantly, how and when such activity may be less than completely functional in this regard. By thinking about curriculum form and content at such abstracted levels, it is easy to forget that real people often act in ways that may be nonreproductive—and sometimes quite consciously so.

We find such realities, in part at least, in the study undertaken by Paul Willis, *Learning to Labor: How Working Class Kids Get Working Class Jobs.*[38] Divided into ethnographic and analytic segments, Willis' book details the interplay between the school and work lives of working-class boys attending secondary school in an industrial town in England. The relationship between this group's culture and the formal experiences and culture of the school is used by the author as an example of how working-class ideology and cultural forms help reproduce class distinctions. In the process, social control is maintained not by the overt intervention of some repressive state apparatus, or any other "outside" coercion, but by the development and solidification of what Antonio Gramsci refers to as cultural hegemony, or that "range of structures as well as values, attitudes, beliefs and morality that in various ways support the established order and the class interests which dominate it."[39] The development of hegemonic control of a citizenry is to be understood as being imposed not by the overt, conscious manipulation of one group by another, but by the dominance of certain ideas, values, and perspectives that saturate people's consciousness while differentially affecting members of particular social and ethnic groups.

"The lads" of which Willis writes form their own counterculture while being immersed within the "official" or dominant culture of the school. They consciously exploit whatever "cracks" or "crevices" they can either discover or create within the existing culture of the school in ways that allow some measure of control over their own lives. The lads' oppositional activity, Willis writes, "is expressed mainly as a style. It is lived out in countless small ways which are special to the school institution, instantly recognized by the teachers, and an almost ritualistic part of the daily fabric of life for the kids."[40]

Another group of students within this secondary school, the "ear'oles" (so termed because of their tendency to just sit and listen), accept and comply with the authority structure and culture of the school; these are the students who at least superficially comply with the rules and regulations of the school. Such students help provide the day-to-day, concrete cultural symbols and artifacts which the lads disdain. The ear'oles' acceptance of school rules and their dress, hair styles, and mannerisms are equated with the established culture of the school, just as such cultural patterns and the formal curriculum become part of a broader perspective felt as distant and alien, and finally rejected, by the lads.

An essential ingredient of the lads' refusal to participate in the official culture of the school is that in a significant sense it is not real for them; it has no relationship to the working-class world which surrounds them, their families, and their friends. The lads respond to school by embracing the more familiar and meaningful cultural forms of the working class while rejecting any notion of intellectual work that the school in part embodies. Here we can see one crucial ideological distinction being formulated and ingrained in the lads' rejection of schooling and school culture. Mental labor and manual labor—"book learning" versus the pedagogy of the shop floor—become separate categories for the lads, and one of the central divisions which sustains their class identity.

Willis' study is important for several reasons and has clear implications for correspondence theories such as those offered in the writings of Bowles and Gintis analyzed above. Willis illustrates how and why such correspondence theories fail in their analysis of reproduction. It is simply not the case that the needs of capitalist production result in the automatic imposition of certain dispositions, personality traits, and ways of thinking on students who acquiesce to and act on such economic needs. At least some important elements of the capitalist workforce are produced in the process of rejecting the skills, propensities, and cultural symbols necessitated by capitalist production and perpetuated by schools; the contradictions built into the lads' penetrations of the official culture serve to solidify social—class standing and working—class ideology. The response of the lads within school gives them strength as members of a valued group while equipping them for employment in work that will ensure the continuation of their class history and social status.

What this implies, in a general way, is that we must see cultural and economic forms as intimately linked and conjoined. These areas are not as separable or isolated as many would have us believe; though thinking of culture as divorced from social relations and economic production may itself serve an ideological function in a society such as ours. That is, it may be politically useful for people to think of especially "high" culture—as encapsulated within the confines of modern aesthetic theory—as abstracted from daily life and social exchange. As Marx said in *The German Ideology*, "the class which has the means of material production at its disposal, has control at the same time over the means of mental production. . . . The ruling ideas are nothing more than the ideal expression of the dominant material relationships, the dominant material relationships grasped as ideas."[41] In Marxist terminology, we must begin to see superstructure and infrastructure not as distinct levels with some causal relationship obtaining between them, but as different aspects of a complex, dynamic social reality. What this means for cultural and aesthetic forms, fundamentally, is that we must view these not as removed from everyday life through the insertion of some form or another of psychological or virtual distancing that ends up focusing on the internal, surface qualities of cultural and aesthetic forms, with the result that aesthetic objects and experiences lose significant portions of their meaning and significance; but as part of the material, productive forces of people's lives and social experience. Ideology is not some abstruse, impenetrable set of theoretical suppositions, but a range of day-to-day activities, perspectives, assumptions, and exchanges that compose social life. "Ideology is not," as Terry Eagleton has argued, "a set of doctrines; it signifies the way men live out their roles in class-society, the values, ideas, and images which tie them to their social function."[42]

Conclusions

The view that schools are meritocratic institutions, "sifting and winnowing" in a fair and unproblematic way that will determine which students succeed and which fail, misses how social currents, economic pressures, and cultural beliefs and distinctions help shape the school curriculum, teaching, and schooling. Analyses and evaluations that only look internally at school practices, focusing on isolated student and teacher behaviors, and presume that decisions about what forms of knowledge and experience are most valuable are apolitical have the effect of normalizing classrooms and curricular offerings. Thinking about achievement and socialization measures as if they provide objective data that are unrelated to external realities is simplistic and deceptive. Evaluating the performance of teachers via external agencies and councils who gauge compliance with "accepted" practices and standards is equally problematic.[43]

What the critical sociological literature tells us, in terms of what schools do and how the curriculum and teaching practices affect educational and social directions, is that we cannot understand just these particular things. We need, instead, to understand how the "external" influences on the school—the economic pressures, political priorities, dominant cultural currents, and ideological perspectives—affect and often shape curricula and teaching practices.

But this is not where this story ends. For many teachers, administrators, students, parents, and others can and do take seriously the contexts in which they live and work. Moreover, they also take stands that oppose conventional ways of thinking about schooling, challenging as a result the social and cultural forces that exert powerful influences on classrooms. There is no guarantee that such challenges will happen in any given school or classroom, of course, just as it is not a "sure thing" that they will be supported if challenges to the status quo are mounted. But teachers, especially working with colleagues in and outside the school, do often make a real difference in the lives of individual students and in articulating a perspective on social justice, power relations, and educational change.[44]

One of the routes we can pursue in trying to create more changes in schools and in establishing ways to create new educational and social directions—ones that will make more and better differences, involves rethinking the nature of aesthetic experiences and the meaning of the arts in society and in schools. Willis' study documents both the material nature of culture and its linkage to ideological commitments. Both these factors need to be further explored in relation to aesthetic symbols and meanings and their political possibilities.

Notes

1. Michael W. Apple and Landon E. Beyer, "Social Evaluation of Curriculum," *Educational Evaluation and Policy Analysis* 5, no. 4 (Winter, 1983): pp. 425–434.

2. Erik Olin Wright, *Class Structure and Income Determination* (New York: Academic Press, 1979), pp. 57–58.

3. It is worth reemphasizing that neither schools nor curriculum are "things," that is, separable objects or entities that can be understood and evaluated independently of other institutions and practices. Rather, they are to be understood within the context of other social realities and cultural patterns which involve complex processes, meanings, and activities that are relatively fluid, changeable, and filled with contradictory tendencies. Thus, while it is convenient to speak of schools and curriculum as more or less autonomous entities, it should be kept in mind that such a shorthand way of thinking about and discussing schools and curriculum can easily be misleading.

4. I do not mean to suggest here that a "functional analysis" of schooling and curriculum, an analysis which posits a simple, uncontested relationship between school practice and the wider society, is adequate or accurate. As will be clear from the analysis presented in this chapter, the relationship between curriculum form and content and pedagogy, on the one hand, and ideology, on the other, is quite complex, oppositional, and contradictory. "Function," then, should not be thought of in this context in any efficient, smoothly running, mechanical sense.

5. See John Dewey, *Democracy and Education: An Introduction to the Philosophy of Education* (New York: The Free Press, 1966).

6. Herbert M. Kliebard, "Persistent Curriculum Issues in Historical Perspective," in *Curriculum Theorizing: The Reconceptualists*, ed. William Pinar (Berkeley, CA: McCutchan Publishing Corporation, 1975), p. 41.

7. Ibid., p. 42.

8. See Landon E. Beyer and Kenneth M. Zeichner, "Teacher Education in Cultural Context: Moving beyond Reproduction," paper presented to the American Educational Research Association, Los Angeles, CA, April 1981.

9. Kliebard, "Persistent Curriculum Issues in Historical Perspective," p. 43.

10. See John Dewey, "The Relationship of Theory to Practice in the Education of Teachers," *National Society for the Scientific Study of Education*, 3rd yearbook, pt. 1 (Bloomington, IL: Public School Publishing Company, 1904).

11. See, for instance, Willard Waller, *The Sociology of Teaching* (New York: John Wiley and Sons, 1932); and Howard Ebmeier and Thomas L. Good, "The Effects of Instructing Teachers about Good Teaching on the Mathematics Achievement

of Fourth Grade Students," *American Educational Research Journal* 16, no. 1 (Winter 1979), 1–16. For critiques of these traditions, see Beyer and Zeichner, "Teacher Education"; and Peter Goldstone, "A Plea for Incompetence," *Philosophy of Education Society Proceedings 1978* (Champaign, IL: Philosophy of Education Society): 44–61. See also Landon E. Beyer, "Teacher Education, Reflective Inquiry, and Moral Action," in *Issues and Practices in Inquiry-Oriented Teacher Education*, ed. B. Robert Tabachnick and Kenneth M. Zeichner (London: Falmer Press, 1991), pp. 113–129.

12. Robert Dreeben, *On What Is Learned in School* (Reading, MA: Addison-Wesley Publishing Company, 1968).

13. See Phillip W. Jackson, "The Daily Grind," in *Life in Classrooms* (New York: Holt, Rinehart and Winston, 1968).

14. Dreeben, *On What Is Learned*, pp. 85–86.

15. Maxine Greene, "The Matter of Mystification: Teacher Education in Unquiet Times," in *Landscapes of Learning* (New York: Teachers College Press, 1978).

16. J. Floud and A. H. Halsey, "The Sociology of Education," *Current Sociology* VII, no. 3 (1958): p. 171.

17. See, for example, Michael W. Apple, *Ideology and Curriculum* (New York: Routledge, 1979), and *Education and Power* (Boston: Routledge & Kegan Paul, 1982); Geoff Whitty, *Sociology and School Knowledge: Curriculum Theory, Research, and Politics* (London: Methuen, 1985); Philip Wexler, *Social Analysis of Education: After the New Sociology* (New York: Routledge, 1990); and John Smyth and Geoffrey Shacklock, eds., *Being Reflexive in Critical Educational and Social Research* (Bristol, PA: Falmer Press, 1998).

18. Samuel Bowles and Herbert Gintis, *Schooling in Capitalist America* (New York: Basic Books, 1976).

19. Ibid., p. 130.

20. Ibid., p. 129.

21. Ibid., p. 132.

22. See, for instance, Apple, *Ideology and Curriculum*.

23. Richard Edwards, *Contested Terrain* (New York: Basic Books, 1979).

24. There are, though, a number of ways in which corporate and smaller economic institutions try to directly influence educational policy and practice. See in this context Alex Molnar, *Giving Kids the Business: The Commercialization of America's Schools* (Boulder: Westview Press, 1996).

25. See, for example, Landon E. Beyer, *Creating Democratic Classrooms: The Struggle to Integrate Theory and Practice* (New York: Teachers College Press, 1996); and Landon E. Beyer and Michael W. Apple, eds., *The Curriculum: Problems, Politics, and Possibilities*, 2nd ed. (Albany: State University of New York Press, 1998).

26. Michael F. D. Young, "An Approach to the Study of Curriculum as Socially Organized Knowledge," in his *Knowledge and Control* (London: Collier-Macmillan Publishers, 1971).

27. Ibid., p. 26.

28. Ibid., p. 32.

29. See, for example, Michael Streibel, "A Critical Analysis of Three Approaches to the Use of Computers in Education," in *The Curriculum*, ed. Beyer and Apple. For "technological advances," see David Noble, *American by Design: Science, Technology, and the Rise of Corporate Capitalism* (New York: Knopf, 1977); and Bill Readings, *The University in Ruins* (Cambridge: Harvard University Press, 1996).

30. Apple, *Ideology and Curriculum*, pp. 36–37.

31. Ibid., p. 37.

32. Basil Bernstein, *Class, Codes, and Control*, vol. 3, *Towards a Theory of Educational Transmissions* (London: Routledge & Kegan Paul, 1975).

33. Ibid., p. 88.

34. Ibid., p. 88.

35. Ibid., p. 94.

36. Ibid., p. 96.

37. Ibid., p. 97.

38. Paul Willis, *Learning to Labor: How Working Class Kids Get Working Class Jobs* (Lexington: D. C. Heath, 1977).

39. Quoted in Madeline Macdonald, *The Curriculum and Cultural Reproduction* (Milton Keynes, England: Open University Press, 1977), p. 69.

40. Willis, *Learning to Labor*, p. 12.

41. Quoted in Frederic L. Bender, ed., *Karl Marx: The Essential Writings* (New York: Harper Torchbooks, 1963), p. 183.

42. Terry Eagleton, *Marxism and Literary Criticism* (Berkeley: University of California Press, 1976), p. 6.

43. See Landon E. Beyer and Jo Anne Pagano, "Democratic Evaluation: Aesthetic, Ethical Stories in Schools," in *The Curriculum*, ed. Beyer and Apple.

44. See Beyer, *Creating Democratic Classrooms*; Michael W. Apple and James A. Beane, eds., *Democratic Schools* (Washington, DC: Association for Supervision and Curriculum Development, 1995); and Ronald E. Butchart and Barbara McEwan, eds., *The Democratic and Emancipatory Potential of Public Education* (Albany: State University of New York Press, 1998).

Chapter 4

The Arts and Social Possibility

Behind the ideas and issues discussed in this chapter is an essentially moral commitment to changing some of the current realities of schooling and the social realities with which they are interconnected. The tendencies of schools to engage in social, economic, and cultural reproduction, and more specifically to emphasize intellectual apathy, linear thinking, respect for authority, isolated and individualizing work, ideologically impregnated views of what it means to be "human," and interpretations and meanings of events that are often partial and ideologically useful in maintaining forms of cultural hegemony, for example, have been well documented.[1] This is not to suggest that schools uniformly do this, or that teachers have consciously sought to provoke such outcomes, or that conscious attempts to do these things are always successful. The work of many dedicated, hard-working teachers has provided evidence of the possibilities of education reversing the tendencies toward intellectual apathy and linear thinking.[2] Yet the dominant structures and processes of schooling—whose knowledge gets taught there, what kinds of evaluative practices and social relations are promoted, the traditions on which we have relied in thinking about curriculum and pedagogy—have often served to promote perspectives and values that are socially and culturally reproductive. Here we will be concerned with ways in which the process of resisting the tendencies toward passivity and submergence can be invigorated, as we formulate alternative visions and practices in the arts, ones that can alter the current realities of schools and the personal, social, and cultural contexts that help shape them.

Aesthetic Experience and Social Realities

Suzanne de Castell has argued that philosophers of education need to ask, "How it is that *philosophical* practice is defined for us, in terms of how such definition is accomplished. . . . It's worth wondering what is it we miss out when we define philosophy of education as we have traditionally done, and it becomes particularly interesting to investigate what it might mean for philosophy of education if our discourses and practices were truly to be redefined in relation to the contemporary material and social conditions within which and in relation to which they are currently being carried out."[3] A question that follows from this inquiry is what sort of aesthetic theory and what kinds of educational activities might help us see the connections between the arts and contemporary material and social conditions and how those conditions might be altered.

A variety of perspectives and actions, ways of seeing and doing, have emerged that seek to open new conceptual and political ground in educational, social, and cultural theory. The current climate may provide a moment for some synthesis or integration of divergent possibilities where this is of value, knowing that difference is a value that frequently makes a difference. Or perhaps the politics of a "radical pluralism" that respects difference—but that appropriately values an at least temporary strategic, synthetic vision that allows for alternative possibilities built upon the possibility of collective interests—may in some way be the only real option we have in a world in which security and certainty are exposed as deception.[4]

The question of how aesthetic meanings may move us to new ways of thinking, and thus new ways of acting, is, of course, part of a larger question about the relationship between aesthetics and the social order. That relationship was effectively denied by the modern aesthetic theories, discussed in chapter 1, that specified how aesthetic experiences are different from more common, day-to-day encounters. Yet clearly there are other important traditions and perspectives that might be offered of this relationship.

In *The Long Revolution*, Raymond Williams says that when trying to understand some past society, we have at our disposal various documents and historical memorabilia.[5] We often acquire these materials in a piecemeal fashion and attempt to formulate an accurate picture of what that society was like. We may learn how that society was organized, how its institutions functioned, what political values and policies it employed, and the like, but these particular systems were seldom viewed as separable and isolated by the living members of that society. Members of any social group normally view their world relatively seamlessly and do not artificially separate its segments for analysis unless such analysis contributes to a greater understanding of the whole. Williams argues that there is always an underlying framework or organization through which these materials and cultural objects are viewed; this framework constitutes a way of life, a mode of existence in its most significant respect. This framework is the lens through which the activities of a society are seen to have particular meanings for its members. It is what Williams has termed the "structure of feeling" of a society or culture. This very potent phrase insightfully captures what is basically an evanescent, informal, unlearned part of a society's intrinsic being or character. Williams says of this concept, "In one sense, this structure of feeling is the culture of a period: it is the particular living result of all the elements in the general organization. And it is in this respect that the arts of a period, taking these to include characteristic approaches and tones in argument, are of major importance"; further, in the arts, "in the only examples we have of recorded communication that outlives its bearers, the actual living sense, the deep community that makes the communication possible, is naturally drawn upon."[6]

Thus, artistic activities and objects within a society reflect and help form a structure of feeling that permeates the whole of that society—its institutions, communication patterns, and the lives of its people in general. There is a dialectical interaction between the nature of a society's institutions and the aesthetic forms and feelings it produces and values. By scrutinizing the art objects of a culture or society we may be able to approximate its structure of feeling in terms of its aesthetic values. In all societies there exists this underlying, dynamic, tacit structure of feeling.

Yet art and the aesthetic not only reflect our values, modes of thought, and structure of feeling, but can inform them and thus radically change our way of life, our very existence as human beings. As Williams has amply demonstrated with respect to dramatic forms as indices of societal change, "complicated as it is by delay, by the unevenness of change, and by the natural variety of responses to change, only some of which achieve adequate communication, the outline surely exists, in which we can see drama, not only as a social act, but as a major and practical index of change and creator of consciousness."[7] Aesthetic forms are important because they signify and encapsulate a society's structure of feeling, and this tacit, underlying way of seeing and responding to one's circumstances contributes to forms of consciousness within a particular social organization.

This structure of feeling points to the ways in which culture—specifically aesthetic forms—needs to be identified as more than objectified, distanced objects disconnected from daily life. Instead, these forms are part of the material processes of social interaction and institutional organization. Not only do structures of feeling go beyond more formal, systematic ideas and beliefs, but this concept itself is "concerned with meanings and values as they are actually lived and felt"; and, since "the relations between these and formal or systematic beliefs are in practice variable (including historically variable)."[8] we need to see in each case how the structure of feeling within a society is part of the historical situatedness of that culture. Within such a framework, we can begin to see how aesthetic meanings are part of the historical and social processes which exist within any society.

Without wanting to suggest that aesthetic experiences are identical to other kinds of experiences and activities, Williams seeks to lessen the estrangement between art and material production, an estrangement which characterizes modern aesthetic theory. By calling the construction of artifacts "creation" rather than understanding them as belonging to the larger, generic class of "production," a separate realm for art is reinforced. As this kind of abstraction progresses, Williams says, "We find ways of neglecting (or of dismissing as peripheral) that relentless transformation of art works into commodities, within the dominant forms of capitalist society. Art and thinking about art have to separate themselves, by ever more absolute abstraction, from the social processes within which they are still contained. Aesthetic theory is the main instrument of this evasion. In its concentration on receptive states, on psychological responses of an abstractly differentiated kind, it represents the division of labour in consumption corresponding to the abstraction of art as the division of labour in production."[9]

Such sentiments represent the antithesis of psychologically oriented attitude theories of aesthetic response. By creating a divergent domain for aesthetic production, removing it from the ongoing social and material processes which constitute any organized social system, the commodification of aesthetic forms becomes easier to overlook or remains unnoticed. To go beyond the processes of commodification and abstraction, Williams says, "we have to reject 'the aesthetic' both as a separate abstract dimension and as a separate abstract function. We have to reject 'Aesthetics' to the large extent that it is posited on these abstractions."[10] As indicated in chapter 2 above, we must understand aesthetic images and meanings as responding to a set of social, historical, and cultural forces that serve to make aesthetic meanings what they are. Understanding the nature of aesthetic response and meaning, in other words, necessitates placing such responses within the larger historical and social contexts within which they occur. They cannot be understood as isolated, extra-social, nonhistorical occurrences to be evaluated and appreciated via the application of specialist, abstracted aesthetic criteria and categories. Rather than utilizing such criteria, we must see aesthetic creation and response as part of the productive, material processes of society. While this emphasis on the material nature of aesthetic by no means negates understanding the various symbolic systems employed in the arts, it is imperative that we see and understand such symbolic systems as part of a particular historical, social milieu.

This perspective requires some awareness of the debate within Marxist theory over the relationship between the economic "base" of society and those ideas and institutions which make up the "superstructure." While the issues involved in this debate have a long history and are exceedingly complex, some understanding of this issue is indispensable for familiarizing ourselves with Williams' view of ideology (one of the components of any "superstructure") and its relationship to culture and aesthetic forms.

Perhaps the most common version of the "base and superstructure" question involves conceiving the base as embodying those economic configurations having to do with the relations of production-relationships between people and the natural environment, which serves as the basis for people's labor, relationships among workers themselves, and relationships between people and the products of their labor. "The base" then becomes concerned with those activities through which work of a particular kind is made possible, social relations develop, and so on. The "superstructure," on the other hand, is often thought of as those social, political, and cultural practices and institutions—and the ways of thinking which attend these—that are somehow caused by the economic activities of society. The disagreements within Marxist theory center on what the relationship is between social-superstructural elements and economic relations of production. In a simplistic formulation of this relationship, we could say that the economic patterns of a society determine in some causal way the social, political, and cultural practices operant in that society. On such a view any change in the base (and *only* a change in the base) will result in a corresponding change in superstructural arrangements and patterns. In this sense the latter can be viewed as "reflections" of those underlying elements composing the base.

Other writers have posited intermediate stages between a simple base/superstructure model as a way of making the linkages a bit less deterministic. Frequently it is said that at least some of these intermediary elements have "partial" or "relative" autonomy from the economic base, so that, for example, cultural patterns and beliefs are not causally determined by economic considerations, while still being influenced by them in some significant way.

The problem with the skeletal base/superstructure model, as well as the more elaborated one, is the assumption that these terms refer to different "areas" or "entities." This, in Williams' view, is a clear misinterpretation of Marx's own thought: "in the transition from Marx to Marxism, and then in the development of expository and didactic formulations, the words used in the original arguments were projected, first, as if they were precise concepts, and second, as if they were descriptive terms for observable 'areas' of social life."[11] Whereas Marx intended "base" and "superstructure" to be primarily relational terms, they became transformed and reinterpreted as if they were one-dimensional, concrete objects and things. Thus what started out as an attempt to explain complex, changing, often contradictory processes and relations in society came to be seen as fixed categories naming separate areas, necessitating the creation of some relationship between these now differentiated aspects of social life. Rather than seeing these as discrete areas or elements, Williams urges us to consider the denotations "base" and "superstructure" as growing out of a common source—namely, the real, social/material activities and interactions of real people.

Just as we need to see aesthetic response as one of a number of important—if nonetheless distinct—material and social processes, so too does the concept of ideology need to be similarly situated within a material, social context. "Ideology" must be understood as part and parcel of lived experience, as forming an integral part of the daily interactions in which we partake.

To understand the relationship between aesthetics and ideology, to see how a structure of feeling is a part of our actual social existence, we must understand aesthetic meanings not as separable from a social/material context but rather as an integral part of that context. Aesthetic meanings and response must be placed in a context shared by other kinds of social meaning, production, and intervention. An example of how this kind of analysis might be undertaken is offered by Williams himself.

In his discussion of "programming as a sequence or flow in television," Williams urges us to consider this cultural form from a perspective that is quite different and insightful.[12] Though we are used to seeing the array of news shows, network productions and specials, and a wide variety of dramatic and sports shows as "main events" interspersed with the various interruptions or commercial distractions, these elements actually constitute a larger totality and help give meaning to this cultural practice. As Williams puts this point, "the real programme that is offered is a *sequence*, or set of alternative sequences . . . which are . . . available in a single dimension and in a single operation."[13] The author claims that the phenomenon of television contains a sequential continuum of events, not a series of discrete visual images and auditory displays which govern our viewing and become interrupted by other messages. The meaning of television lies in the totality of the experience rather than in time intervals defined by programs that we see as particular and individuated.

This perspective is, of course, seldom consciously entertained by television viewers; we watch television, on the surface at least, to see a specific production that is being broadcast. Yet Williams maintains that "many of us sit there (in front of the television set, for several hours in succession), and much of the critical significance of television must be related to this fact."[14] Commenting on this critical significance, Williams writes, "The apparently disjointed 'sequence' of items is in effect guided by a remarkably consistent set of cultural relationships: a flow of consumable reports and products, in which the elements of speed, variety and miscellaneity can be seen as organising: the real bearers of value."[15] With respect to news reporting, such bearers of value become more transparent: "At one level the average length of a news item is in effect determined by the time-unit of attention which the commercials have established. Nothing is at all fully reported . . . Yet the flow of hurried items establishes a sense of the world: of surprising and miscellaneous events coming in, tumbling over each other, from all sides."[16] Thus it is in the flow of television, the sequence of programs, commercial and other interruptions, newscasts, specials, and so on, that the cultural messages of TV take on meaning. That meaning is, moreover, dialectically related to the way that viewers think about the experiences which make up their world.

Williams' analysis of the images and messages communicated through television can serve as one model of the kind of undertaking that is required if we are to take the material nature of culture, art, and ideology seriously. By focusing on how the material characteristics of television as a cultural form are related to the development of forms of consciousness that are ideologically laden, Williams demonstrates both how aesthetic meanings are part of a larger process of material and social production and how they are related to the dominance of ways of thinking in society. The fragmented experience that television both represents and helps further becomes endemic in a society that increasingly strives toward greater and greater occupational and social specialization. In addition, fracturing experience into small, isolated units has the effect of making any larger, more connected social understandings much less likely. In effect, particularizing experience in the way that increases specialization and fragmentation works against any larger-scale understandings of the interactive workings of contemporary society. In this way, the fragmentation, of images, symbols, and experiences, that occurs in television production is helpful in perpetuating ways of thinking that assist in continuing current social and political arrangements and patterns. By linking the aesthetic and cultural practices of television with social processes, we are presented with the sort of analysis that attempts to see aesthetic meanings as a particular form of material production, and as related to forms of consciousness that are often ideologically beneficial. The kind of fragmentation, particularization, and commodification of aesthetic forms that Williams documents in the case of television can only be appreciated and evaluated within such a material, historical framework. Another example of how such a perspective can be brought to bear on art forms is offered by John Berger in his provocative book *Ways of Seeing*.[17]

While Williams analyzes television, Berger focuses on the historical and social influences upon, and consequences of, the visual arts, especially painting and drawing. In particular, he correlates changes and developments in painting with changes in economic form. At the same time, he sees the usual exclusive emphasis on various aesthetic categories (visual rhythm, harmony, contrast, and so on) as mystifying these more social and economic dimensions of the visual arts. In considering two paintings by Frans Hals, *Regents of The Old Men's Alms House*, and *Regentesses of The Old Men's Alms House*, Berger quotes at length a more traditional, compositional analysis of the paintings. This traditional reflection upon Hals' paintings focuses on the use of shading and various qualities of line, qualities which produce a certain kind of internal rhythm, contrast, and the like. After citing this compositional approach to art appreciation, Berger says: "The compositional unity of a painting contributes fundamentally to the power of its image. It is reasonable to consider a painting's composition. But here [in the aesthetic analysis previously cited] the composition is written about as though it were in itself the emotional charge of the painting. Terms like 'harmonious fusion,' 'unforgettable contrast,' reaching 'a peak of breadth and strength' transfer the emotion provided by the image from the plane of lived experience to that of disinterested art appreciation.' All conflict disappears. One is left with the unchanging 'human condition'; and the painting considered as a marvelously made object."[18]

The compositional analysis of the Hals paintings critiqued by Berger offers insight into the sort of formalist approach to aesthetics fostered by modern aesthetic theories. We see how a formal, single-minded focus on such formal elements as "harmonious fusion" and "unforgettable contrast" undermines other ways of thinking about painting and alternative renderings of aesthetic significance. In considering paintings as "marvelously made objects" through a disinterested aesthetic, paintings become mere comments on a generalized, and hence nearly meaningless, "human condition." It is not so much that such interpretive analyses are wrong or inaccurate as that they tend to tell us so little of substance about the emotional and personal significance of art in general and individual works of art in particular. In the process, artistic expression and aesthetic response become trivialized, and much of the meaning of these activities lost.

Berger's analysis is helpful in clarifying why this is so. He begins by pointing out that Hals, a man of eighty at the time these paintings were commissioned, was himself destitute, with most of his life having been spent in debt. During the year in which these two paintings were produced (1664), for example, Hals obtained three loads of peat from charitable sources; without this he would have frozen to death. The regents and regentesses depicted in the two paintings were in fact responsible for the administration of such charities. Berger uses this information as an aid in interpreting and giving meaning to the figures depicted in the paintings. He uses the actual painted figures, their gestures and demeanor, as evidenced within the painting, as the basis for arriving at his interpretation. Yet his appreciation of these works of art goes beyond merely the surface features that are enumerated through a compositional analysis. He supplements our understanding and interpretation of the paintings with the biographical information about the painter indicated above. That is not, however, the only "evidence" which can be used to interpret these paintings. The "seduction" of such paintings, that is, the feeling spectators often have that they know the personality traits and habits of the people depicted, Berger says, "is nothing less than the paintings working upon us. They work upon us because we accept the way Hals saw his sitters. We accept it as it corresponds to our own observation of people, gestures, faces, institutions. This is possible because we still live in a society of comparable social relations and moral values. And it is precisely this which gives the paintings their psychological and social urgency. It is this—not the painter's skill as a 'seducer'—which convinces us that we can know the people portrayed."[19]

Seeing a painting as only formally interesting is inadequate. Berger insists that it is the conflict between the painter and his subject that we must deal with as art appreciators: "In this confrontation the Regents and Regentesses stare at Hals, a destitute old painter who has lost his reputation and lives off public charity; he examines them through the eyes of a pauper who must nevertheless try to be objective, i.e., must try to surmount the way he sees as a pauper. This is the drama of these paintings. A drama of an 'unforgettable contrast.'"[20] By placing the paintings within both a historical and material context, the latter of which is understandable not because of some nebulous connection with the "human condition" but because we live in and recognize a culture imbued with similar social and economic relationships, the meaning of Hals' paintings is expanded; their significance is made more intense. At the same time, the paintings become more conflictual. Such a process of contextual positioning virtually breathes new life into more usual or compositional analyses offered by art critics. It extends these paintings' value for us as a result, by extending the range of meanings thought legitimate and valuable. Instead of the usual mystification that typifies a good deal of art criticism, Berger's approach allows us to see that "Hals was the first portraitist to paint the new characters and expressions created by capitalism. He did in pictorial terms what Balzac did two centuries later in literature."[21] By utilizing a different approach to aesthetic experiences, Williams and Berger are able to provide an expanded significance for art.

The theoretical postulates of Raymond Williams, as well as their application to television and painting in his and Berger's analyses, indicate the many ways in which aesthetic meanings need to be understood as connected to social processes and the development of forms of consciousness. We have seen how a structure of feeling is a vital part of the ways in which people view and understand themselves, their relation to other people and institutions, and their society in general; how both ideological and cultural forms must be seen as on a par with those other material processes that take place in any social organization; and how forms of consciousness—ways of making sense and acting within the world—need to be understood within this process of ideological construction.

The dispassionate attention to the surface features of aesthetic experiences viewed disinterestedly focused on the pursuit of an objective approach to the arts, and on the distancing of emotional responses that would "devalue" the meaning of the experience. In hoping that such bracketed observations would create forms of knowledge akin to that available through logic, aestheticians advocating this way of engaging the arts believed that even the existence of an actual object was not necessary for aesthetic contemplation. The development of such a modern, distanced, objectified perspective is traceable to the modern era and the perspectives and directions associated with it. It is also traceable to a set of convictions and presuppositions that have historically been affiliated with masculinist points of view. A number of important alternatives to those points of view have been articulated by women artists and critics.

Forms of Feminist Aesthetics

In *A Room of One's Own*, Virginia Woolf wanders through the apparently pacific environs of Oxbridge University, appreciating both the natural and cultural wonders that compose that environment.[22] She recalls essays on the works of Milton and Thackeray, essays that suggest that not a single word could be changed for the better in these classics. She considers whether, contrary to such views, any changes in the original manuscripts might actually have been made by either author, and decides to investigate, realizing the library in which these texts are housed is only a few hundred yards away. Upon discovering that entrance to this library is prohibited to those unaccompanied by a fellow of the college or a letter of introduction, Woolf is forced to leave. She writes, "That a famous library has been cursed by a woman is a matter of complete indifference to a famous library. Venerable and calm, with all its treasures safely locked within its breast, it sleeps complacently and will, so far as I am concerned, so sleep forever. Never will I wake those echoes, never will I ask for that hospitality again, I vowed as I descended in anger."[23]

Later that day, after having the kind of luncheon normally reserved for the privileged and having considered the value of libraries, churches, food, and wealth, Woolf reconsiders what she has seen and heard; she wonders, ". . . what effect poverty has on the mind; and what effect wealth has on the mind; and I thought of the queer old gentlemen I had seen that morning with tufts of fur upon their shoulders; and I remembered how if one whistled one of them ran; and I thought of the organ booming in the chapel and of the shut doors of the library; and I thought how unpleasant it is to be locked out; and I thought how it is worse perhaps to be locked in."[24]

Instead of seeking an assumed safe haven, set off from the world of ugliness, manipulation, and mechanical repetition that composes a seemingly ever larger portion of our daily lives, we must recontextualize the aesthetic as a force existing within the intersections of familial, social, ideological, and historical currents and actions that compose central elements of our actual and possible lives.

Yet how are we to develop a language to substitute for the masculinist views of detachment, objectivity, and neutrality, views that have shaped our modern understanding of art through such mechanisms as attitude theories of aesthetic experience. In *Sex, Class, and Culture*, Lillian S. Robinson discusses what it means for an idea to be "bourgeois" in more or less traditional Marxist terms,[25] citing *The German Ideology* as explaining how the strands of power intersect within a class that rules in both an ideational and a material sense.[26] She follows that citation with the observation that "Italian adolescents have expressed the same view somewhat more colorfully: 'How could a young gentleman argue with his own shadow, spit on himself and on his own distorted culture while using the very words of that culture?' " [27]

We have tried often to utilize the meanings, images, and metaphors of the ways of thinking we seek to transcend within the very act of criticism. Our own language can indeed be a powerful prison house. Such is the situation in a good deal of current writing in educational and aesthetic-cultural theory, and one that may be mitigated, at least in part, by a feminist aesthetic.

There are several important respects in which work in feminist aesthetics has altered our understanding of the value of the arts. Not the least of these is the extent to which the historical exclusion of women's (and other marginalized groups') art and the misrepresentation of women and others, either through silence or absence or more overt means, has been recognized and has caused a response. In terms of realizing the potential of a feminist aesthetic, one course of action involves recognizing this possibly liberating potential of women's expression.

This concern for recognizing women's art is related to the question, explored by Rosalind Coward, of whether *women's* works of art are necessarily *feminist* works of art.[28] As Michele Barrett asks,

> Is the recovery of women's artistic work of the past an integral part of our developing feminist project, or merely a sentimental resuscitation of marginalia better left in the obscurity to which establishment criticism has consigned it? What do we gain by elevating traditional crafts such as embroidery and knitting to the status of art objects and hanging them in galleries? What is the meaning of an art exhibition where the objects displayed are kitchen utensils or the careful record of a child's upbringing? How should we react to art that claims to be based on a "female language" or on an artistic rendering of the female body and genitalia? In what sense might these various imaginative comments on women's experience be seen as "feminist" art? Is a work of art feminist because the artist says it is, or the collective who produced it announce their feminist principles of work?[29]

The study by Judy Chicago, *The Dinner Party*, perhaps epitomizes some of the issues surrounding the questions posed here. For Barrett, the Chicago exhibit in its portrayal of Virginia Woolf, for example, is less than illuminating: "There [Woolf] sits: a genital sculpture in deep relief (about four inches high) resting on a runner of pale lemon gauze with the odd blue wave embroidered on it. Gone is Woolf's theory of androgyny and love of gender ambiguity; gone the polemical public voice; gone the complex symbolic abstractions of her writing. I found this exclusive emphasis on genitalia, and the sentimentality of the trappings, a complete betrayal."[30] Unlike Coward, however, Barrett concludes that while not all women's art is feminist art, whatever feminist art is must be a subset of women's experience—a shared experience of patriarchal oppression.

Another possibility for understanding and valuing a feminist aesthetic entails recognizing the double-sided partiality in male views of the canon, and suggests that we need to reconsider not only the basis of aesthetic significance but also its gender determinants. Such an approach promises to significantly widen what is considered art, and to the extent that it is successful it could reform both aesthetic sensitivities and aesthetic education. This seems to be a guiding perspective in Andreas Huyssen's essay "Mass Culture as Woman."[31] In considering the problems associated with "saying I" for the woman writer, Huyssen says, "Given the fundamentally differing social and psychological constitution and validation of male and female subjectivity in modern bourgeois society, the difficulty of saying 'I' must of necessity be different for a woman writer. . . . The male, after all, can easily deny his own subjectivity for the benefit of a higher aesthetic goal, as long as he can take it for granted on an experiential level in everyday life."[32] In redefining subjectivity and recognizing the gender determinants of varieties of it, we challenge the definitions of valued art, definitions that center on masculine cover-ups of a subjective objectivity.

Yet a third possibility for a feminist aesthetic is one that raises questions about the very nature of "an artistic tradition," and the basis upon which only some creative actions are labeled "art." This provides a more fundamental challenge to mainstream assumptions about art, as it undermines the hierarchical structures upon which artistic canons depend. Yet the problem with such a view is the tendency to deny any criteria with which we might distinguish among works of art as to their value—however that might be conceptualized and in spite of the intellectual and practical difficulties of coming to some agreement on what this value might be.

In terms similar to those just utilized in considering the possible value of a feminist aesthetic, Elaine Showalter nicely summarizes the varieties of feminist criticism: "The intellectual trajectory of feminist criticism has taken us from a concentration on women's literary subordination, mistreatment, and exclusion, to the study of women's separate literary traditions, to an analysis of the symbolic construction of gender and sexuality within literary discourse. It is now clear that what we are demanding is a new universal literary history and criticism that combines the literary experiences of both women and men, a complete revolution in the understanding of our literary heritage."[33]

The threat of homogenization and marginalization is always present in any reputedly universalizing theory, as many people writing within postmodernism have pointed out.[34] While such threats are real and must be continually guarded against, responses must be rooted in social and political activities that attack injustices; these require some form of political solidarity. To the extent that postmodernism fosters an insularity of discourse and a particularity of knowledge claims, it undermines efforts to act in the name of social justice—efforts that require concerted, collaborative actions combining global and local sensitivities.[35] These efforts can be enhanced, as well, by emphasizing the integration of aesthetic and other activities, necessitating what Judith Barry and Sandy Flitterman-Lewis describe as "the need for a feminist reexamination of the notions of art, politics, and the relations between them, an evaluation which must take into account how 'femininity' itself is a social construct with a particular form of representation under patriarchy."[36]

This understanding of a feminist aesthetic raises the crucial question of cultural politics and its role within feminist criticism and practice. Simply put, what are the politics of cultural production, distribution, and appreciation and what is the connection between feminist art and politics?

I would argue, with Barrett, that while not all women's art is feminist, all feminist art is related to a common experiential background. The question of cultural politics is then immediately complicated by the realities of class, ethnicity, race, sexual orientation, and so on. If feminist art is necessarily based upon the socially constructed experience of being a woman, how divergent can that experience be (given membership in other groups, differing value commitments and priorities, a range of historical situations, and so on) and still be identified as essentially *women's* experience? Under what circumstances, within what contexts, and with what theoretical perspective does gender have the centrally organizing role in the experience of women? What do we do with experiences that involve women, but not centrally as gendered subjects, or that involve men as something other than subjects who are fundamentally gendered, but where there are other, perhaps compelling similarities, commonalities, and possible political alliances, for example, those surrounding race, ethnicity, age, or class.[37]

I want to suggest that it may be possible to construct a critical aesthetic theory that, in including several strands within its boundaries, does not homogenize the important differences among them, but that can serve as a force for political action. Such a cultural politics must be able to move toward social and cultural transformation, and this certainly assumes a commonality of purpose among the protagonists and always poses a threat to diversity and authenticity among "the others." [38]

Cultural Politics and the Arts

One problem with basing any approach to the arts on a particular fund of experiences—even if we can decide what the elements of commonality that create such experiences are to be—is that such an approach, if left unexamined and unclarified, can easily become an individualistic, essentially psychological domain. Left out is a consideration of the structural pressures that shape and reshape that experience. An awareness and critical understanding of such structures is essential if we are to develop a critical aesthetic that carries with it the possibilities of social change. As Barry and Flitterman-Lewis explain, "In evaluating . . . types of women's art, our constant reference point will be the recognition of the need for a theory of cultural production as an armature for any politically progressive art form. . . . Every act (eating an orange, building a table, reading a book) is a social act; the fundamentally human is social. Theory enables us to recognize this and permits us to go beyond individual, personally liberating solutions to a socially liberated situation. . . . Theory, as a systematic organization of the range of cultural phenomena, can produce the tools for examining the political effectiveness of feminist art work." [39]

The authors go on to develop a four-part typology of women's art, a typology that is interesting and useful. This typology identifies artworks: (1) that assume a female essentialism and result in the "glorification of an essential female art power,"[40] for which the Judy Chicago exhibit provides one example; (2) that view "women's art as a form of subcultural resistance,"[41] which would typically include women's crafts as a kind of counterculture; (3) that are submerged in or entirely outside of patriarchal forms of expression, including women artists who see themselves as "separatists" and those who are nonfeminists, seeking acceptance from patriarchy; and (4) that situate "women at a crucial place within patriarchy which enables them to play on the contradictions that inform patriarchy itself."[42] This final segment of women's art recognizes the socially constructed nature of "woman" and "women's art," the role of discourse in those processes of production, and the intersection of multitudinous social practices. Further, the authors elaborate, "Activism alone in women's art has limited effects because it does not examine the representation of women in culture or the production of women as a social category. We are suggesting that a feminist art evolves from a theoretical reflection on representation: how the representation of women is produced, the way it is understood, and the social conditions in which it is situated."[43]

This effort to produce a dialectical, participatory, situated feminist aesthetic "implies a break with the dominant notion of art as personal expression, re-situating it along the continuum connecting the social with the political and placing the artist as producer in a new situation of responsibility for her images."[44] This sort of feminist art moves us beyond the categories of disinterestedness and isolation, providing clues to what might be central to such art beyond its being a part of collective "women's experience." It also distinguishes itself from other sorts of feminist aesthetic theory—the study of women's exclusion from the canon, the development of women's own artistic traditions that dismiss canonical views altogether—as it seeks to understand the situatedness of art so that it can further the alteration of those very situations.

An emphasis on the socially constructed nature of art, and its links with other institutions and actions, lies close to the center of a socially sensitive, material, productive aesthetic. A social theory of aesthetics informed by feminism and a feminist theory of aesthetics informed by a non-reductionist social theory provide a possibility for personal and structural transformation through the arts.

This view is based upon the belief that an organic unity that gives voice to aesthetic value, political possibility, and personal liberation is theoretically defensible and practically feasible. Such a unity must transcend the often critiqued but still deeply embedded dichotomies of reason/emotion, objective/subjective, public/private, and productive/reproductive, dichotomies that we have inherited, in part, from patriarchy. Within the view that I am urging, two propositions are especially important: first, that, in representing or expressing situations or themes, all art contains within it an at least implicit way of seeing, constructing, and making sense of the world, of communicating a vision of what life is or could become—and therefore both hides and discloses political and social visions. Such visions may be harder or easier to discern, given a particular work's complexity and symbolism and the extent to which the members of the audience share symbolic and experiential reference points and are open to aesthetic forms that challenge conventional ways of seeing. Second, I am claiming as well that no liberation movement can be totally or exclusively personal, individuated, or psychological, as important as these elements frequently are. Nor can "the social" and "the personal" be conceived as separable, reified categories with autonomous existences and points of reference. If "art" and "politics" cannot be isolated, neither can "personal" and "social" change which the arts can help forge.

The sort of critical aesthetic theory that is consistent with an integration of the personal/political, and of art/politics, sees the arts as an important aspect of social and personal life, connected with material, structural, and personal relations that are complex, dialectical, and sometimes oppositional—relations that extend well beyond the encounter with a particular work of art. By locating women's experience within this complex set of constructs, and by seeing the arts as a basis for both understanding and transforming the socially constructed definitions of women, art, and politics, a critical theory of feminist aesthetics may be realized, a theory that can help alter our consciousness, our schools, and our social situations.

In rejecting the notion of art as socially removed, ideologically neutral, and impersonal, we challenge some of the most important, dominant traditions in European, male-dominated aesthetic theory. As a project with politically transformative possibilities, the construction of a critical, socially conscious alternative theory of aesthetics must be able to promote collaborative, collective pursuits that work toward the overthrow of relations of dominance in a society characterized by oppressive and unequal relations of power and domination; such an aesthetic theory must also be broad enough, and open enough, to foster the personal expressions of people denied a voice in society and the mainstream artistic community as we generate a different sort of community within which diversity and points of intersection are respected. We cannot afford people who are "locked in" or "locked out." If the arts divorced from a social context are empty, the aesthetic without a sensitivity to personal voice must surely be blind.

What does this perspective imply for the re-creation of aesthetic education that is tied to the development of a critical consciousness and to social change? There is an array of cultural, ideological, and social realities within which students (and adults, too, of course) develop their orientations and values, which often conflict with the very values and practices required for the development of a critical consciousness that can be furthered by a reconceived aesthetic. The treatment of women and girls in a variety of texts and institutions, the violence depicted on television and in other media (as well as the violence witnessed by many children everyday as they make their way from home to school and back again), the racism in open view in many families, neighborhoods, and communities, and the systemic nature of the oppression visited on the poor, people of color, and women may well affect the forms of consciousness that students bring to schools. And these forms of consciousness will also shape the very student interests that progressives have long thought central to include within the curriculum. We are bombarded by ideologically laden representations that reflect dominant social interests and often become sedimented into students' consciousness; the resulting hegemony may create interests that, when expressed, encode sentiments and priorities that are the very antithesis of what is required for significant social change.

Ignoring those hegemonic beliefs and practices is not possible. Pretending that such beliefs are inconsequential results in superficial forms of student participation within which significant educational experiences do not take place, since ideas remain disconnected from those core values and perceptions that affect the meaning of school and social life. Even when students listen attentively to teachers' and texts' discussions of the horrors and injustices of racism, for example, their commitment to racial equality, social justice, and sensitivity will be only verbal if we do not help them make connections between their own experiences and daily interactions and the ideal of equality. This is a fundamental problem associated with the use of textbooks and other sanitized and dislocated forms of knowledge, inquiry, and curricula.

Conclusions

One of the things that I believe is centrally required in order to create alternative, critical, material, feminist, and social—aesthetic theories is the incorporation of forms of popular culture—television programs, movies, music, video productions, texts, video games, and so on—into the curriculum of our schools so that developing an understanding of the meaning and influence of such works becomes an important part of schooling. Helping students develop a critical, analytical, reflective attitude toward those forms of popular culture in which they are caught up but which are not often formally or carefully analyzed, and which are usually seen as nonacademic or otherwise inappropriate for the public schools, is central if we are to encourage not only the *expression* but also the *critical evaluation*, of those forms. At the same time, an emphasis on certain moral values—equality, tolerance, respect for human life and the need for peace, a commitment to some notion of a common good, for example—will not be significant for students unless they can come to understand the meanings of such lofty ideals within their own day-to-day lives. If we are to facilitate in schools some notion of an ethical culture to which an altered form of aesthetic education might powerfully contribute, it is important that the personal, social, and political implications of moral values for our lives and actions, in and out of school, become a part of the curriculum. This might be encouraged by the production of student forms of popular culture that connects what are often considered more distant moral imperatives and the real-life, flesh and blood experiences of children—in and out of school. The arts, as these capture both the meaning of common events and the possibilities for alternative ways of life, might well make lasting contributions to this effort. They would certainly lead to critiques of the processes of social and cultural reproduction as analyzed in chapter 3.

The arts can, through the imaginative rendering of people, events, values, places, feelings, and ideas, help disclose worlds that are not yet in place, and thus serve as a force to bring about their creation. This is the political and moral promise of art, a promise to be fulfilled not through a narrow instrumentalism, but through its efficacy in helping us reflect on and transform our ways of life, our experiences, and our personal and social being. This is only a potential value of the aesthetic experience, of course, and not one that is currently widely held. If it is to become a reality, we must continue to develop an aesthetic theory that goes beyond an abstracting Formalism and an isolating psychologism—one that places the arts as a material, productive force within the moral values, everyday lives, and personal and social interactions of people. Such a theory, and the experiences it makes possible, might indeed help us respond to the forms of oppression and alienation in the world, even as we invigorate public school classrooms so that they actively resist the reproductive forces of society.

Notes

1. See Philip W. Jackson, *Life in Classrooms* (New York: Holt, Rinehart and Winston,1968); Elizabeth Vallance, "Hiding the Hidden Curriculum: An Interpretation of the Language of Justification in Nineteenth-Century Educational Reform," ed. in *Curriculum and Evaluation*, ed. Arno A. Bellack and Herbert M. Kliebard, (Berkeley: McCutchan, 1977); Michael W. Apple, *Ideology and Curriculum* (London: Routledge & Kegan Paul, 1979); Kenneth A. Sirotnik, "What You See Is What You Get: Consistency, Persistency, and Mediocrity in Classrooms," *Harvard Educational Review* vol. 53, 1 (February 1983); and Larry Cuban, *How Teachers Taught: Constancy and Change in American Classrooms, 1890–1980*, 2nd ed. (New York: Teachers College Press, 1992).

2. See, for example, Landon E. Beyer, *Creating Democratic Classrooms: The Struggle to Integrate Theory and Practice* (New York: Teachers College Press, 1996); Sheldon Berman and Phyllis La Farge, eds., *Promising Practices in Teaching Social Responsibility* (Albany: State University of New York Press, 1993); George H. Wood, *Schools That Work: America's Most Innovative Public Education Programs* (New York: Penguin Books, 1992); and Barbara Brodhagen, Gary Weilbacher, and James Beane, "What We've Learned From 'Living in the Future,'" in *The Curriculum: Problems, Politics, and Possibilities*, 2nd ed., ed. Landon E. Beyer and Michael W. Apple (Albany: State University of New York Press, 1998).

3. Suzanne de Castell, "Textuality and the Designs of Theory," in *Critical Conversations in Philosophy of Education*, ed. Wendy Kohli (New York: Routledge, 1995), pp. 253–254.

4. See David Plotke, "Marxism and Democratic Theory," *Dissent* (Summer 1989), pp. 343–349.

5. Raymond Williams, *The Long Revolution* (London: Chatto and Windus, 1961).

6. Ibid., p. 48.

7. Ibid., p. 273.

8. Raymond Williams, *Marxism and Literature* (Oxford: Oxford University Press, 1977), p. 153.

9. Ibid., p. 154.

10. Ibid., p. 156.

11. Ibid., p. 77.

12. Raymond Williams, *Television: Technology and Cultural Form* (New York: Schocken Books, 1974).

13. Ibid., p. 87.

14. Ibid., pp. 95–96.

15. Ibid., p. 105.

16. Ibid., p. 116.

17. John Berger, *Ways of Seeing* (New York: Penguin Books, 1972).

18. Ibid., p. 13.

19. Ibid., p. 14.

20. Ibid., p. 15.

21. Ibid., p. 16.

22. Virginia Woolf, *A Room of One's Own* (New York: Harcourt, Brace and Company, 1929).

23. Ibid., pp. 11–12.

24. Ibid., p. 40.

25. Lillian S. Robinson, *Sex, Class, and Culture* (New York: Methuen, 1978).

26. Karl Marx and Frederick Engels, *The German Ideology* (Moscow: Progress Publishers, 1976).

27. Robinson, *Sex, Class, and Culture* p. 5,6.

28. Rosalind Coward, "Are Women's Novels Feminist Novels?" *Feminist Review* Issue no. 5, 1980, pp. 53–64.

29. Michele Barrett, "Feminism and the Definition of Cultural Politics," in *Feminism, Culture and Politics*, ed. Rosalind Brunt and Caroline Rowan (London: Lawrence and Wishart,1982), pp. 42–43.

30. Ibid., p. 45.

31. Andreas Huyssen, "Mass Culture as Woman: Modernism's Other," in *Studies in Entertainment: Critical Approaches to Mass Culture*, ed. Tania Modleski (Bloomington: Indiana University Press, 1986).

32. Ibid., p. 190.

33. Elaine Showalter, "The Feminist Critical Revolution," in her *The New Feminist Criticism: Essays on Women, Literature, and Theory* (New York: Pantheon Books, 1985), p. 10.

34. See, for example, Michel Foucault, *Power/Knowledge: Selected Interviews and Other Writings, 1972–1977*, ed. Colin Gordon (New York: Pantheon Books, 1980); Henry Giroux, "Postmodernism and the Discourse of Educational Criticism," *Journal of Education* 170, no. 3 (1988); Richard Rorty, *Contingency, Irony, and Solidarity* (New York: Cambridge University Press, 1989); and Elizabeth Ellsworth, "Why Doesn't This Feel Empowering? Working through the

Repressive Myths of Critical Pedagogy," *Harvard Educational Review* 59, no. 3 (1989).

35. Landon E. Beyer and Daniel P. Liston, "Discourse or Moral Action? A Critique of Postmodernism," *Educational Theory* 42, no. 4 (1992).

36. Judith Barry and Sandy Flitterman-Lewis, "Textual Strategies: The Politics of Art-Making," in *Feminist Art Criticism: An Anthology*, ed. Arlene Raven, Cassandra L. Langer, and Joanna Frueh (Ann Arbor: UMI Research Press, 1988).

37. See Landon E. Beyer and Daniel P. Liston, *Curriculum in Conflict: Social Visions, Educational Agendas, and Progressive School Reform* (New York: Teachers College Press, 1996).

38. See Beyer and Liston, "Discourse or Moral Action?"

39. Barry and Flitterman-Lewis, "Textual Strategies," p. 88.

40. Ibid., p. 89.

41. Ibid., p. 91.

42. Ibid., p. 94.

43. Ibid., p. 94.

44. Ibid., p. 97.

Chapter 5

Art, Schooling, and Social Action: Toward New Possibilities

This chapter provides the outline for an alternative conception of curriculum theory and development in the arts based on the view that cultural production and social action can become significant parts of educational, and especially classroom, activity. A revitalized vision of the aesthetic, one that incorporates a critical and productive conception of the relations between art and society, provides an emancipatory perspective with which educational practice may be conceived and constructed. It is my hope that both the activities of those employed by schools and the philosophical understandings that guide curriculum theorists ultimately can be strengthened in the process of formulating this alternative direction for the arts and education.

A central undertaking in this context is the articulation of a relationship between the arts and the larger realms of social interaction. In one form or another, defining the contours of this relationship occupies the majority of this chapter. In beginning with a short summary of the modern tradition in aesthetic theory described in chapter 1, and the alternatives discussed in chapter 4, we will see how the perspective of a Marxist aesthetic offers a counter to the modern tradition, and how it enhances a more productive theory of artistic creation and appreciation. Finally, I briefly indicate how a way of thinking about and acting on behalf of the social and political significance of the arts can be created, a way that heightens our own (and our students') social consciousness, political sensitivity, and sense of personal power. These directions offer a promising perspective from which to explore alternative educational practices in the arts.

Art and Social Life

Recall that among the defining characteristics of classical aesthetic theory is the tendency to move the focus of attention regarding the possibilities of appreciation from the art object itself toward a consideration of the psychological states or conditions which must prevail within the appreciator. Rather than some quality or component of the work of art being necessary for an aesthetic experience to be possible, meaningful, or of value, the dispositional traits of the percipient became the basis for these aesthetic possibilities. This requires the adoption of an "aesthetic attitude" that separates art from other experiences.

The effect of this tradition has been to abstract aesthetic experience from our more usual or common interactions, giving it a life of its own. Yet certain core problems seem endemic to classical aesthetic attitude theories, problems which admit of no clear or obvious solution.

First, in their more strictly interpreted versions, these theories simply do not explain the level of significance—the depth of feeling, emotion, and thought—that artworks are capable of provoking in their admirers. Understanding the formal, surface qualities of Coppola's *Apocalypse Now*, for example, simply does not disclose the full significance of this work.[1] When we abstract from our experience of this film those social, political, and personal events that inform the meaning of the images that flow across the screen, it loses an important part of its aesthetic significance and power.

Second, what these approaches to works of art miss, in a sense, is the content of the aesthetic experience, as can be seen in a variety of Formalist theories that are derivative of the classical tradition.[2] Attitudinal theories result in virtually contentless experience, leaving the percipient to savor only those presentational features immediately perceptible during the actual encounter with the artwork. A sustained analysis of how aesthetic content may go beyond such a delineation of presentational features is disallowed.

Third, as a result, something of importance is lost about the nature of aesthetic value when attitude theories form the basis for aesthetic experience. This set of theories shares an essential conceptual orientation which severely limits how aesthetic objects may prove valuable. Essentially, these theories reduce aesthetic value to an appreciation of the artwork's formal structure, valuing only the depiction of surface features which exist (the qualities of line, shading, brush stroke, symmetry, etc., in painting, for example).

In separating art from life, in severing the ties among aesthetic experience, ethical deliberation, and social conduct, we sacrifice its personal and political potency, relegating it to a mere decorative or ornamental function.[3] One clear alternative to this tradition can be found in a Marxist aesthetic.

Aesthetics and Materialism

There is a danger, especially bothersome in the case of a seminal thinker like Karl Marx, that his particular views on aesthetic matters will be interpreted apart from the larger corpus of writing that forms Marx's collective work. Yet to fully understand the nature of Marx's writings on aesthetics, one needs to see how they are part of that larger body of writing. This requires a more extended analysis than is possible here.[4] Thus, the contextualization of Marx's writing on art in this essay will be necessarily brief, undertaken following a review of his more specific ideas on the arts and aesthetic experience.

Attempts to arrive at the true, faithful, or unmediated version of Marx's general thought are notorious and controversial. The commitment to faithfully recounting Marx's own view is especially problematic in the case of the arts since one is obliged to admit early on that neither Marx nor Engels provided anything like a fully developed aesthetic theory. This lack of a comprehensive theory of art is itself something of an enigma. For Marx evidently had an abiding interest in the arts, especially literature, from the beginning of his formal schooling (e.g., his study of the history of art and literature at the University of Bonn and of aesthetics at the University of Berlin). This interest continued throughout his life. Marx reportedly knew portions of Shakespeare's plays from memory, and as late as 1857 he sought to comply with an offer from the *New American Cyclopedia* for an article on aesthetics—an undertaking that was, however, not to be completed.[5] Whether we subscribe to the view that the lack of a systematic aesthetic theory is due to "the fact that Karl Marx had more urgent tasks on his hands,"[6] or to some other set of circumstances, the fact remains that no treatise on aesthetics was ever formulated by Marx of the sort that might parallel his analysis of political economy.

One of the first events in Marx's professional life relevant to piecing together a materialist view on art concerns his reaction to attempts at censorship of the press. Rather than reacting simply to the specific question of press censorship, Marx saw this issue as intimately related to the status of literature generally in bourgeois society. The division of labor and other changes brought about by a capitalist economy promoted commodification and commodity fetishism. Because of the fetishistic quality of social life, activities and objects of all kinds—including works of literature and the arts—became regarded as commodities, to be "purchased" and "used" as such.[7] Within such a society, "the bourgeois . . . tries to use in literature, the same criterion which he applies to sugar, leather, and bristle. He considers freedom of the press a 'thing,' and this is contrary to its character."[8] In reducing literary works to the status of things, their value becomes transformed and debased. As Marx put this, "the exchange value of a palace can be expressed in a certain number of boxes of shoe blacking. On the contrary, London manufacturers of shoe blacking have expressed the exchange value of their many boxes of blacking, in palaces."[9] In a society suffused with and enamored by the exchange value of commodities, the role and value of art objects becomes mutated.

The tendency for literature to be reduced to the status of a commodity for trade, thus, propelled Marx's reaction to attempts at censorship. In addition to the view that literary works are nothing more than goods to be bought and sold on some market, commodity fetishism propounds the view that literature is a means of subsistence for the writer. Yet literature, Marx wrote, "is an end in itself, so little is it a means for [the writer] and for others that he sacrifices his existence to its existence, when necessary. . . . The freedom of the press consists primarily in not being a trade. The writer who degrades it by making it a material means deserves, as punishment for this inner slavery, censorship; or rather this existence is already his punishment."[10] Further, "is a press true to its character, is it free when it degrades itself to the level of a trade? A writer naturally must earn money in order to be able to write, but under no circumstances must he live and write in order to earn money."[11]

The corrupting influence of the process of commodification in bourgeois society is at the heart of Marx's critique here, lest the writer become a tradesperson and the production of literature only a means for his/her survival. For Marx there were evidently two distinct types of writers and literary works. Whereas Milton "produced *Paradise Lost* for the same reason that a silk-worm produces silk," another author will "fabricate books under the direction of his publisher"; as a result, the latter author's work is "from the outset subsumed under capital."[12] Literature, to be faithful to its nature, must be organically conceived and carried out rather than undertaken as a means of capital accumulation.

Marx's first article on freedom of the press, written in 1842, captures an important duplicity involved in the Prussian government's attempt to reintroduce and enforce state censorship.[13] In its censorship instructions, the government had said that, partly for the sake of national unity, criticism of its measures must be "well intentioned and not spiteful or malevolent."[14] In this rationale Marx saw the pitting of one class against another, in spite of official declarations to the contrary. Marx said of the censorship instructions, "A law like that is not a law of the state for the citizenry, but a law of a party against another party. The tendentious law cancels the equality of the citizens before the law. . . . One person may do what another person may not do, and not because the latter lacks the objective capability for the action . . . but rather because his intentions are suspect."[15] Criticizing attempts at instituting a broadened conception of censorship, Marx exposed the presumed attempts at promoting patriotism and unity as the pitting of one group, the state as represented by the censors, against the people as represented by the press.

Marx also protested the censorship edict because it mandated a grayness or dullness of style, as well as a flattening of what was considered appropriate content. In the disallowance of inquiry which fails to aim at "serious and restrained pursuit of truth,"[16] Marx saw an unjustifiable constriction of what constitutes the "pursuit of truth." He provides a rather poetic taunt of the government's censorship edict: "Every dewdrop in the sun glitters in an infinite play of colors, but the light of the mind is to produce only one; only the official color, no matter in how many individuals and in which objects it may be refracted. The essential form of mind is brightness and light, and you want to make shadow its only appropriate manifestation. It is to be dressed only in black, and yet there are no black flowers. The essence of mind is always truth itself, and what do you make of its essence? Restraint. Only a good-for-nothing holds back, says Goethe, and you want to make the mind a good for nothing?"[17] The truly creative spirit, in pursuing truth, does not flourish in some neutral, aseptic realm where passion, color, and commitment are excluded. The genius, the impassioned writer of true literature, sees and reveals life in all its colors, using language, images, and concepts that, contrary to the edict of 1842, must be unrestrained.

Literature and the other arts are to be the agents, then, in the pursuit of truth, a role which places a premium on discovering and deciphering those realities wherein truth presumably resides. Rather than thinking about the arts as vehicles for the exploration and expression of aesthetic form—as in modern aesthetic theory—Marx saw literature as committed to an impassioned, unrestrained search for truth, a search compromised by the censor.

Yet what constitutes the arena for this search, and the resulting emphasis on realism, in Marx's view? A number of the important principles of materialist art in the Marxian sense are to be found in the responses of Marx and Engels to the drama *Franz von Sickingen* by Ferdinand Lassalle.

This drama deals with a sixteenth-century German uprising in which the insurgent peasants are led by the petty nobility, as personified by von Sickingen. After a few cursory comments on some formal features of this work, Marx comments more substantively on the conflict represented in it. Marx admired Lassalle's attempt to draw analogies between sixteenth- and mid-eighteenth-century Germany, but he was critical of the explanation for von Sickingen's actions. Rather than von Sickingen failing in his role because of some flaw in his character, as Lassalle apparently intimates, Marx declares that the tragic hero "went under because it was as a knight and a representative of a moribund class that he revolted against the existing order of things. . . . The fact that he began the revolt in a guise of a knightly feud means simply that he began it in a knightly fashion. Had he begun it otherwise he would have had to appeal directly and from the outset to the cities and peasants, i.e., precisely to the classes whose development was tantamount to the negation of the knights."[18]

The tragedy of von Sickingen occurs not because the hero was somehow personally defective or incapable, but because he represented the collision of modern ideas with the material interests of a reactionary class, interests which capture his real social roots. Continuing his criticism of Lassalle's drama, Marx says that rather than giving the aristocratic representatives of the insurrection so much play, the author ought to have allowed "the representatives of the peasants and the revolutionary elements in the cities" a more active role.[19] What Marx is essentially suggesting, hence, is that Lassalle's drama did not fully or accurately reflect the actual historical currents which created the revolutionary situation discussed in the drama. The author's treatment of the event was not, in short, sufficiently realistic.

Engels' criticism of *Franz von Sickingen*, while on the whole more laudatory than Marx's, follows the same outline. In recalling a specific scene in the drama, Engels echoes Marx's recommendation that greater emphasis be given to the peasants: "In accordance with my view of drama, which consists in not forgetting the realistic for the idealistic, Shakespeare for Schiller, the inclusion of the sphere of the so wonderfully variegated plebian society of that day would have supplied . . . entirely new material for enlivening the drama, an invaluable background for the national movement of the nobility in the foreground, and would have set this movement in the proper light."[20] After discussing another possible modification in Lassalle's work, it becomes clearer what the "proper light" might consist in: "This is," Engels admits, "only one way in which the peasant and plebian movement could have been incorporated into the drama. At least ten other ways of doing this just as well or better are conceivable."[21] What Engels is suggesting is a reworking of *Franz von Sickingen* so that the central historical movements of the peasants, movements which underlie and shape this tragedy, could be more clearly delineated and exposed. Again, we see an emphasis on realism within art as a key feature of Engels' treatment of literature. Central to the view of literature discussed above is a concept with wide-ranging application (and misapplication) within a Marxist aesthetic, the notion of typicality. We may understand "typicality" as Marx' and Engels' view that, "progressive literature had to reflect truthfully the deep-lying, vital process of the day, to promulgate progressive ideas, and to defend the interests of the progressive forces in society. The modern term 'the Party spirit' in literature expresses what they understood by this. They felt that the very quality that was lacking in Lassalle's play—the organic unity of idea and artistry—was the *sine qua non* of genuinely realistic art."[22] To express typicality is to capture, in artistic form, the main social and historical currents in the era depicted in a way that captures their essential—if hidden—nature and qualities.

By connecting this emphasis on realism and typicality with Marx's insistence on a sense of commitment that accompanies those who seek the truth, we have the view that "only partisanship in art . . . can give the modern artist that precision and concentration of will, that creative 'one-sidedness,' which is essential to genuine art."[23] Capitalist society conceives of literature as a commodity and a means (something to be marketed as a product and produced as if it were a trade). It also places limitations on literary activity through censorship, reflecting the disguised pitting of one class against another (the result of which is a barrenness of content and style). On the contrary, the true literary genius, whose writing represents an organic pursuit of the truth, depicts the typical characters within real circumstances and situations, displayed in all their various colorations.

Further insight into a materialist aesthetic is provided by Marx and Engels in their first collaborative work, *The Holy Family*. This book deals in part with a critical appraisal of Eugene Sue's *The Mysteries of Paris* and its analysis by Szeliga, a Left Hegelian. More generally, *The Holy Family* can be seen as a treatise against "speculative aesthetics" as a whole since many of the authors' comments apply to "not only Sue's novel but also the entire moral and aesthetic creed of the 'dominant personality' of the nineteenth century—the bourgeois."[24]

Marx and Engels begin their discussion of Sue's novel and Szeliga's reaction to it with a more generic discussion of "speculative construction in general." The authors say that, starting from real material objects such as apples, pears, and strawberries, the general idea "fruit" may be imagined. The speculative philosopher will suppose that this general idea somehow captures the essence of being of these separate physical entities and that thus, the fruit is itself a real, objectively existing entity separable from the speculator herself/himself. Apples, pears, and so on, are perceived as mere instances of the real subject, fruit. Individual apples and pears thus become "no more than semblances whose true essence is 'the substance'—fruit."[25] Having postulated an idealized category to which individual objects are mere semblances, the speculative philosopher now faces something of a problem—how to move from the ideal category to the material object. He/she must explain why there is such diversity among objects which, ideally, belong to the same category. To do this, Marx and Engels say, the idealist proclaims that "Fruit [is] not dead, undifferentiated, motionless, but a living, self-differentiating, moving essence. . . . The different ordinary fruits are different manifestations of the life of the 'one Fruit'; they are crystallizations of 'the Fruit,' itself."[26] Thus real, physical objects, which we perceive through our senses as objectively existing, become mere signifiers of an allegedly deeper, abstracted reality. Real fruits, in this scheme of things, become the miraculous creation of the imaginary powers of the mind; they are created out of abstract reason which is considered external to the person involved in this idealized activity, as the product of an absolute subject.

This same sleight of hand occurs, Marx and Engels argue, in idealist aesthetics. In the case of *The Mysteries of Paris,* the "real relations" of law and civilization are dissolved into the category of "mystery." This idealist category then, like the category of fruit in the previous illustration, becomes a self-existing subject that is incarnated in real situations, actions, and experience. Two examples will indicate how this process of transformation occurs in Sue's novel.

During the course of the novel's progression, there is a transition from the "low world" to the "aristocratic world" through the figure of Rudolph. The disguises that Rudolph has at his disposal allow him to move about freely in the lower strata of society, just as the title of prince permits him access to aristocratic society. As Marx and Engels say of one aspect of Rudolph's transition, "On his way to the aristocratic ball he is by no means engrossed in the contrasts of contemporary life; it is the contrasts of his own disguises that he finds piquant. He informs his obedient companions how extraordinarily interesting he finds himself in the various situations."[27] The variability of Rudolph's disguises, their apprehension as one aspect of the Idealist characterization of mystery, becomes the guiding spirit behind this transition from one world to the other; the realities of contemporary life go unnoticed and unexpressed. The latter are transformed into the necessary background, within which abstract mystery unfolds, rather than being central to the content of Sue's novel.

The novelist's treatment of sensuality represents another speculative construction. Marx and Engels tell us that "it is not sensuality which is presented as the secret of love, but mysteries, adventures, obstacles, fears, dangers, and especially the attraction of what is forbidden."[28] Countess MacGregor, another character in Sue's literary work, becomes "a person of abstract reason. Her 'ambition' and her 'pride,' far from forms of sensuality, are born of an abstract reason which is completely independent of sensuality."[29] In the view of Marx and Engels, true sensuality—inspired by "the rapid circulation of the blood" and "the nerve currents which connect the organ . . . of sensuality with the brain"—becomes transformed into another aspect of mystery within this Idealist novel.[30] Thus, for the critic Szeliga, "dancing" (another Idealist category, since it does not denote a specific dance but only dance in general) is perceived as "the most common manifestation of sensuality as a mystery."[31]

In both the above examples—Rudolph's use of disguises and Countess MacGregor's representation of a pseudosensuality—it is not the real flesh and blood experiences of people in concrete social situations that are elaborated upon by the novelist, but the Idealist categories that they speculatively represent: not the lived experience of lower-class and aristocratic people, but the ability of Rudolph to move among them by adopting various disguises which contribute to the development of the mystery; not the actual elements of human sensuality, but their embodiment of other categories and aspects of mystery. It is the latter which become the center of Sue's novel and Szeliga's criticism of it. Speculative construction and imagined categories are center stage for the novelist operating within an Idealist aesthetic framework; social, historical conditions and concrete experience have little place. Commenting on the distinction between an Idealist aesthetic and the criticism leveled against it by Marx, Lifshitz says, "The self-development of sensuous, concrete reality, or its subordination to an alien force: fight or submission; such in the final analysis is the fundamental distinction between the aesthetic—philosophical ideas of Marx and those of Szeliga and Sue."[32]

Realism, typicality, and the depiction of actual occurrences in real situations characterize the central tenets of the view of Marx and Engels on literature and art. Literature must capture the central social and historical trends of the time, must depict the real material conditions of the day rather than use them as a backdrop for the exploration of some set of abstract categories, and must reinforce or propel progressive ideas. To capture such social and historical trends in their progressive guise is not, however, to reduce the political value of art to any sort of proselytizing. As previously noted, the organic unity of artistic excellence and political sensitivity lies behind the authors' notions of typicality and realism in the arts. Whereas "tendency literature" was used to describe certain politically biased art by the Young Germany movement, Engels states that this term is used by him in another way: "The tendency," Engels says, "must be born of the situation and the action themselves without our attention being expressly drawn to it."[33] In a correspondence addressed to a writer, Engels says, "I am far from believing that you are at fault for not having written an authentic Socialist novel, a tendency novel as we Germans call it, promoting the author's own political and social views. That is not at all what I meant. The more carefully concealed the author's opinions are, the better it is for the work of art."[34] Art is not an arm of political propagandizing, but a vehicle for the expression and elucidation of real situations and events, within which one's political and social views are, of necessity, exemplified.

What can we conclude regarding a possible Marxist aesthetic theory, one that combines Marx's comments on the arts with his general theoretical constructs? What is the relationship between art and social life for Marx?

First, we should recognize the peculiarity of the latter question for the methodology of historical materialism generally. For it asks us to determine how the categories "art" and "society" may be superimposed on actual lived experience and human action, a request that Marx and Engels would no doubt reject as an example of Idealist construction. There is no universal, abstract relationship between "base" and "superstructure."[35] Rather, there are particular artistic works which exist within specific sociohistorical circumstances, which exhibit various relations, and which, in general, follow certain tendencies.

Second, a Marxist aesthetic theory must be cognizant of the prescriptive nature of art as discussed above in the authors' insistence on realism and typicality in art. While rejecting political proselytizing as the essence and purpose of art, Marx and Engels repeatedly point to the necessity of creating works which typify the development of social and historical forces. In their criticism of Lassalle's *Franz von Sickingen* and Sue's *The Mysteries of Paris*, for instance, they repeatedly insist that literature typify the important elements of social life; yet this typicality is not to be indulged at the expense of artistic integrity or aesthetic excellence.

Third, in rejecting the notion of literature as a commodity, a means, and a part of commercial trade, a Marxist aesthetic theory proclaims the importance of an impassioned, partisan pursuit of truth. The truth that is possible for literature to pursue is, of course, partly revealed in Marx and Engels' emphasis on typicality. In addition, their opposition to Idealist construction in general, and in the arts in particular, mandates the "development of sensuous, concrete reality." As seen in their more general views regarding historical materialism, the artist must begin with real people in actual situations and conflicts rather than seek to illustrate some speculative, Idealist category such as mystery or insurrection, for example. The work of art must deal with particular interactions of those involved in actual activities and yet somehow capture their sociohistorical essence, thus ascending "from earth to heaven."

Fourth, while a Marxist aesthetic stresses the typification of actual events within concrete historical circumstances, and in this way places value on the progressive nature of art within a historical materialist framework, at least the more vulgar forms of Socialist Realism are a one-sided misinterpretation and simplification of Marx's thought. Such interpretations seize upon a selective portion of his views while effectively discounting others. They highlight the insistence on realism without recognizing the complexity of typicality in the broad sense; stress the importance of progressive content while forgetting the essential Marxian unity of such content and aesthetic excellence; reduce cultural activity to an epiphenomenon, a reflection of the base, a view which glosses over the complexity of notions of "uneven development" and dialectical relations in Marx's thought; and reduce art to "tendency writing" or political propaganda, a view rejected by Marx and Engels in their own writing on art. As one commentator has pointed out, "Vulgarized dogmatic views on the character of the link between art and politics are profoundly alien to the Marxist-Leninist understanding of art. A truthful and diversified representation of reality cannot be replaced by any didactic illustration of political slogans. Such substitution cannot but lead to a belittling of artistic truthfulness and hence undermine art's social impact. The socio-political significance of progressive art is determined by its truthfulness, its convincing reflection and profound revelation of the leading trends to be observed in the life of society."[36]

Fifth and last, a definitive, unassailable version of a Marxist aesthetic is at best evasive and probably impossible to conceptually pin down. There do appear to be, however, a range of possibilities that legitimately fall within the framework outlined above. Those views which stress the importance of searching for the truth by depicting actual experience in its typical configurations and complexities, in the process combining progressive content with artistic mastery, would seem to characterize something central about the nature of art in a Marxist aesthetic. Works of art can profoundly illuminate the major currents of social life; in evoking progressive images of social import, they provide a means of expression to some of our most important political acts.

The view that the arts are an important aspect of social life, connected with material interests and realities within a multitude of complex dialectical, and even contradictory, relationships, forms a striking counterpoint to classical aesthetic theory. How might this view affect the possibilities for aesthetic education within schools?

Aesthetic Theory and Educational Practice

In many respects, recent and current educational situations in the United States seem hardly supportive of new directions for aesthetic education. With the nearly obsessive concerns of the "back to basics" movements in the last decade or so, and now a revitalized emphasis on standards for teacher education and the public schools,[37] the arts are frequently perceived as an educational frill, to be curtailed or eliminated altogether in times of fiscal uncertainty. Reports on the status of American schools have also been mixed in their analysis of the role of the arts in public education. The Carnegie Commission tells us: "Now, more than ever, all people need to see clearly, hear acutely, and feel sensitively through the arts." Such practices "are no longer just desirable. They are essential if we are to survive together with civility and joy."[38] The authors of *The Paideia Proposal*, on the other hand, include "the fine arts" as integral to the body of organized knowledge which all students are to acquire.[39] At the same time, this group also says that while works of art may be dealt with in seminars where discussion of Socratic dialogue dominates, "they need an additional treatment in order to be appreciated aesthetically—to be enjoyed and admired for their excellence."[40] The report goes on to stress the importance of the performance aspects of the arts as well. *The Paideia Proposal* appears to lend support to certain aspects of classical aesthetic theory, in insisting on a particular mode of aesthetic appreciation, while at the same time emphasizing the traditional reliance on the creation of aesthetic artifacts within art education.

A Nation at Risk, the report of the National Commission on Excellence in Education, offers perhaps the bleakest vision of the role of the arts in education. The commission makes little mention of the arts in its analysis, excluding them from what it calls "the new Basics." It suggests merely that "the high school curriculum should also provide students with programs requiring vigorous effort in subjects that advance students' personal, educational, and occupational goals, such as the fine and performing arts and vocational education."[41] *A Nation at Risk,* then, relegates the arts to personalized, vocational, and occupational functions, on the periphery of the secondary school curriculum. It also adopts what appears to be an instrumental role for the arts, and perhaps a quasi-commodified one.

In sum, the recent past seems not to offer the sort of fertile ground from which new approaches to the arts and aesthetic education might flower. Even the occasional support evidenced for the arts in schools seems to hearken back to the vision of aesthetic experience which, as we saw earlier, is both conceptually and socially wanting.

Yet there are some signs that support for some artistic events in schools is substantial. For example, in a survey conducted in 1981, 70 percent of the respondents expressed support for arts education in schools on a full-credit basis. In addition, public expressions of support for the teaching of art actually increased between 1975 and 1981, just as the "back to basics" movement was gaining momentum. Again, in 1981, 75 percent of those surveyed favored regular financing of arts courses in the public schools.[42]

While such public support for arts education seems to offer promise, two other phenomena reflect mitigating social and economic circumstances which may undermine such expressions of support. First, financial information on who attends performing arts events is rather interesting, to say the least. In 1978, the United States median income was $14,476. The same year, the median income of those who visited art museums was about $18,000, while for opera goers the figure was $21,000. At the same time, over 80 percent of the art museum audience had attended college while those whose education stopped with high school composed only 5 percent.[43] These sorts of factors support the view that there exists in the United States a "cultural elite," whose levels of income, status, education, and leisure time combine to make the experience of art an exclusive, privileged, class-based activity. Second, there is an apparently general presumption that art appreciation is made possible or enjoyable because of native talent, and is not dependent upon education or preparation. As Laura Chapman reports in her recent book, this attitude is even shared by the cultural elite: "What is striking about the cultural elite is their reluctance to acknowledge that formal education in art is really essential for one to enjoy and understand art. Equally striking is their belief that the creation of art hinges on talent more than on training . . . these attitudes would be harmless enough if it were not for the fact that the cultural elite is not just a social class defined by statistics; increasingly, it has become a well-organized lobby seeking to influence national and state policies on the arts and arts education."[44] At the same time that art appreciation has become the province of a privileged class, the view that it does not require training, acquired sensitivity, and educated judgment is entrenched in our culture.

These tendencies are hardly surprising. Given the major tenets of classical aesthetic theory, the creation of a cultural elite that can partake in distanced, personally removed experiences is understandable. Because the fine arts tend to be "lifted above the stream of life," they have become the almost exclusive domain of those with appreciable wealth, power, and status. Indeed, the appreciation of aesthetic productions then becomes itself a mark of social status and privilege.

The notion that education in the arts is incidental to their appreciation and evaluation also lends support to the notion that art constitutes an elitist domain. For if art appreciation is possible primarily because of some inherent capacity on the part of only some of the populace, and if this capacity remains relatively unaffected by formal preparation, those who lack this alleged capacity will remain excluded from the domain of art. Moreover, since large segments of the population in fact remain excluded from the art world, we have the makings of a self-fulfilling prophecy regarding legitimate appreciation experiences. Limited by both a perceived lack of "naive talent" and a lack of exposure to the arts in their personal lives, the majority of citizens soon learn to discount art as a life force.

The reintegration of aesthetic value and social conduct outlined in our discussion of a Marxist aesthetic can provide one important counter to the sort of elitism fostered by contemporary approaches to the arts and aesthetic education. If we can incorporate such a perspective into aesthetic education, moreover, we may work toward cultural shifts that could propel larger social changes as well.

What I want to stress is the rejection of that separatist notion that characterizes the place of art in classical aesthetic theory. As Raymond Williams has expressed this, "we have to reject 'the aesthetic' both as a separate abstract dimension and as a separate abstract function. We have to reject 'Aesthetics' to the large extent that it is posited on these abstractions."[45] Instead, based on the view that aesthetic forms are one of several types of material productions, I want to urge recognition of the arts as one sort of lived experience, as part of the social totality from which creation and appreciation, as generic human processes, spring. This does not mean that aesthetic production activity—any more than, say, the material production of automobiles—is identical to the production of political party platforms. Yet from a more global perspective, since social life is composed of multifaceted, historically variable, and personally complex sets of processes, we may be able to carve out a space for aesthetic understanding as a productive force in its own right.

The changes necessary for this to take place within educational institutions are numerous. First the distinction between the "fine arts," on the one hand, and the "popular arts," or popular culture, on the other, must be seen as a spurious one. We have tended to place the former in special arenas—museums, institutes, and galleries. This helps ensure their separation from the rest of social life for many of us. Conversely, we tend to denigrate crafts as somehow unartistic, or at least on a lesser aesthetic plane as compared with Renaissance painting, opera, or ballet. The logic of the analysis of aesthetic forms as productive, fundamentally social and moral phenomena presented here entails the legitimation of the popular arts as of a piece with other forms of artistic expression.

Second, the separation of art in schools—as an elective, frill, or "special subject"—needs to be overcome. This entails not only the increased availability of courses in the arts, but a change in their orientation as well. Arts courses frequently tend to emphasize the performance or constructive nature of art—as exemplified in the creation of paintings, drawings, poetry, dramatic performances, and so on. While such creative ventures are obviously crucial for aesthetic education, it is equally important for students to develop appreciative and evaluative capacities with respect to the arts. That is, not only do the arts serve as a vehicle for the expression of one's own ideas, emotions, and perspectives, but they also create opportunities for investigating the perspectives and values of others.

Third, and related to the importance of developing appreciative capabilities, an important part of broadening the significance of the arts is tied to their communicative potential. While works of art can be regarded from a number of vantage points, it is their capacity to communicate a particular point of view, set of values, or perspective on the world that is most telling if we are to realize their social and ethical connotations. Through a variety of symbolic arrangements, they communicate something to audiences, something that can enhance, modify, or transform the way we see and understand ourselves, others, and existing social arrangements. Paying attention to the communicative nature of aesthetic forms means, then, understanding how they make a statement about some aspect of our own and others' lived experiences.

Fourth, inasmuch as works of art provide a kind of communicative agency, their latent connection to our actions outside the aesthetic encounter must be emphasized. Stated differently, "the self-contained aesthetic encounter" must itself be seen as unsustainable. It is crucial that students see the aesthetic image, social consciousness, and moral action as conjoined. There are at least two possible avenues for this expanded perception. On the one hand, the aesthetic image can become a crystallized vision of what is true, good, or proper—a representation of society, personal relationships, or political practices in what is regarded as their proper light. Such visions offer alternative conceptions of what ought to be, conceptions that, in their illumination and insight, may prove existentially provocative. On the other hand, works of art can provide a critique of current situations and predicaments that challenge the accepted order of things. Now in practice these two possibilities often coincide: the affirmative image emerges with the critique of current situations, or the vision of alternatives implies a grounding for a revised aesthetic vision to become incorporated into schools. Our students need encouragement to use aesthetic forms to illuminate or challenge contemporary issues (the patterns of sexism, racism, or social class exclusion; the atrocities of hate crimes, violent, often gunshot-ridden conflict; other forms of personal violence; and war, for example). Their visions of justice and fairness may become the framework for artistic ventures: they may explore them with the insight provided by symbolic forms which the arts provide.

Fifth, this revised conception of aesthetic education entails a withering of the divisions between the arts and other curricular areas. Not only do we need to infuse the arts with greater social and moral significance, but we need to investigate the aesthetic components of the language arts, social studies, the humanities, and the natural sciences.[46] Integrating aesthetic concerns and possibilities into the other curricular areas of schools is, of course, fraught with peril because it is all too easy to regard the arts as an instrumentally useful tool with which to articulate preconceived ideas from the sciences and humanities—e.g., the occasional visual display of an abstracted idea or concept, the use of arts as depicting central themes, etc. Instead of such instrumental uses of aesthetic forms, what I am urging is the development of our awareness of how scientific, social, and humanistic enterprises all have embedded aesthetic components or aspects. For example, we might show how the patterns of geometric shapes in nature have both mathematical and aesthetic qualities or we might demonstrate how the development of historical trends is related to developments in the arts of a particular culture. The basic notion here is to increase our understanding of how aesthetic, humanistic, and scientific matters are intertwined.

Sixth, more attention needs to be paid to the aesthetic qualities of teaching and evaluation generally.[47] We have been obsessed with quantitative, technical, and individualistic forms of pedagogy and evaluation, to the detriment of other modes and approaches.[48] Both as teachers and teacher educators, we need to uncover the aesthetic dynamics of our interaction with others and how we conduct evaluation studies.[49]

The aim of these proposals is the reintegration of aesthetics into social life and the rejuvenation of the aesthetic image so that its social, moral, and political import may become manifest. This process will require a greater sensitivity to the aesthetic qualities of all experience; a revised theory of aesthetic experiences, one that contextualizes their creation and significance; and a commitment to utilizing such experiences in schools to critique current realities and to promote new ways of seeing, knowing, and doing. In the end, this process will necessitate and help evolve a revised educational and social order within which the arts—as perhaps the highest forms of human achievement—can flourish.

Notes

1. See D. W. Prall, *Aesthetic Judgment* (New York: Crowell, 1929).
2. See, for example, DeWitt H. Parker *The Principles of Aesthetics* (Boston: Silver, Burdett, 1920); and Stephen C. Pepper, *Principles of Art Appreciation* (New York: Harcourt, Brace, 1949).
3. Landon E. Beyer, "Aesthetic Theory and the Ideology of Educational Institutions," *Curriculum Inquiry* 9, no. 1 (1979).
4. Good introductions here include Lee Baxandall and Stefan Morawski, *Marx and Engels on Literature and Art* (St. Louis: Telos Press, 1973); and Mikhail Lifshitz, *The Foundations of Marxist Aesthetics* (Moscow: Progress Publishers, 1977).
5. Baxandall and Morawski, *Marx and Engels*, p. 5.
6. Lifshitz, *Foundations*, p. 7.
7. See the extended analysis of the concept of commodification in Walter Benjamin, "The Work of Art in the Age of Mechanical Reproduction," in his *Illuminations* (New York: Schocken Books, 1969), pp. 217–251; and John Berger, *Ways of Seeing* (New York: Penguin Books, 1972).
8. Lifshitz, *Foundations*, p. 51.
9. Ibid., p. 52.
10. Ibid., p. 52.
11. Ibid., p. 51.
12. Karl Marx, *Theories of Surplus Value* (Moscow: Progress Publishers, 1963), p. 401.
13. Karl Marx, "Comments on the Latest Prussian Censorship Instruction," written in February 1842 for the *Deutsche Jakrbucher,* edited by Arnold Ruge, published in 1843 in the Swiss *Anekdota* when *Jakrbucher* was censored and forced to stop publication. See *Writings of the Young Marx on Philosophy and Society,* Lloyd Easton and Kurt H. Gudda, eds. (Garden City, NY: Doubleday, 1967).
14. Ibid., p. 79.
15. Ibid., p. 80.
16. Ibid., p. 70.
17. Ibid., p. 71.
18. Marx and Engels, *On Literature and Art* (Moscow: Progress Publishers, 1976), p. 99.

19. Ibid., p. 100.

20. Ibid., pp. 105–106.

21. Ibid., p. 197.

22. Ibid., p. 26.

23. Lifshitz, *Foundations*, p. 59.

24. Ibid., p. 67.

25. Marx and Engels, *The Holy Family* (Moscow: Progress Publishers, 1975), p. 68.

26. Ibid., p. 69.

27. Ibid., pp. 73–74.

28. Ibid., p. 77.

29. Ibid., p. 78.

30. Ibid., p. 77.

31. Ibid., p. 79.

32. Lifshitz, *Foundations*, p. 74.

33. Henri Arvon, *Marxist Esthetics* (Ithaca, NY: Cornell University Press, 1973), pp. 36–37.

34. Ibid., p. 37.

35. See Raymond Williams, "Cultural Theory," in *Marxism and Literature* (Oxford University Press, 1977).

36. Avner Zis, *Foundations of Marxist Aesthetics* (Moscow: Progress Publishers, 1977), p. 66.

37. See Linda Darling-Hammond, Arthur E. Wise, and Stephen P. Klein, *A License to Teach: Building a Profession for Twenty-First Century Schools* (Boulder: Westview Press, 1995); Interstate New Teacher Assessment and Support Consortium, *Model Standards for Beginning Teacher Licensing and Development: A Resource for State Dialogue* (Washington, DC: Council of Chief State School Officers, 1992); National Council for Accreditation of Teacher Education, *Program Standards for Elementary Teacher Preparation* (Washington, DC: National Council for Accreditation of Teacher Education, 1999); National Commission on Teaching & America's Future, *What Matters Most: Teaching for America's Future* (New York: National Commission on Teaching & America's Future, 1996).

38. Ernest L. Boyer, *High School: A Report on Secondary Education in America* (New York: Harper and Row, 1983), p. 98.

39. Mortimer J. Alder, *The Paideia Proposal: An Educational Manifesto* (New York: Macmillan, 1982), pp. 22–24.

40. Ibid., p. 31.

41. National Commission on Excellence in Education, *A Nation at Risk* (Washington, DC: U.S. Government Printing Office, 1983), p. 26.

42. Laura H. Chapman, *Instant Art, Instant Culture: The Unspoken Policy for American Schools* (New York: Teachers College Press, 1982), p. 6.

43. Ibid., pp. 171–172.

44. Ibid., p. 8.

45. Williams, "*Marxism and Literature*," p. 156.

46. See, for example, *Reading, the Arts, and the Creation of Meaning*, ed. Elliot W. Eisner (Washington, DC: National Art Education Association, 1978); Peter Abbs, *English within the Arts* (Toronto: Hodder and Stoughton, 1982); Masha Kabokow Rudman, *Children's Literature—An Issues Approach* (Toronto: D. C. Heath and Company, 1976).

47. See Elliot W. Eisner, *The Educational Imagination* (New York: Macmillan, 1979); and Maxine Greene, *Landscapes of Learning* (New York: Teachers College Press, 1978).

48. Michael W. Apple and Landon E. Beyer, "Social Evaluation of Curricu*lum,*" *Educational Evaluation and Policy Analysis* 5, no. 4 (Winter, 1983).

49. See Landon E. Beyer and Jo Anne Pagano, "Democratic Evaluation: Aesthetic, Ethical Stories in Schools," in *The Curriculum: Problems, Politics, and Possibilities*, 2nd ed., ed. Landon E. Beyer and Michael W. Apple (Albany: State University of New York Press, 1998).

Chapter 6

Aesthetic Experience for Teacher Preparation and Social Change

Possible roles for aesthetic experience within educational institutions are rather diverse and, with varying emphases, are discussed with some frequency by those concerned with educational policy and curriculum planning.[1] The view that the arts have an important place within a variety of educational settings is often expressed and accepted, at least rhetorically. Support for artistic endeavors in higher education is associated with a variety of allegations: that they compose one of the core areas within the liberal arts tradition, that they are crucial for the development of personal and cultural sensitivities, or that they form a crucial segment of Western civilization and thus must be preserved and transmitted to succeeding generations. Analogous testimonials have been provided by those working within the public schools, though here the arts curriculum is for the most part an elective rather than a required subject and tends to be seen in terms of the production of artifacts, to the detriment of appreciative and evaluative possibilities.

Yet laudatory portrayals of the arts are not always reflected in school practice. Currently several factors seem to work together to dilute the potential significance of aesthetic experience within schools. First, at the elementary level, either arts instruction tends to be undertaken by specially trained art instructors, with classes meeting infrequently and in isolation from other school activities and subjects, or such instruction is smuggled into a curriculum with focal concerns on reading, various forms of skill development, and mathematics. The result, in both cases, is a sense of curricular isolation and insulation that degrades aesthetic value. Insofar as the arts are seen as "specials," "frills," or nonacademic and "play-full," they suffer a loss of educational status and defensibility in the eyes of students and teachers—a loss legitimated by the allocation of resources and time in many elementary classrooms. Second, courses in the arts in secondary schools, also typically electives, are often seen as ancillary to the central purposes of a high school education. Since secondary schools are increasing their emphasis on the so-called academic subjects, especially as prerequisites for entrance into college, arts education may be a casualty of the competition for credentials. Third, the current general aura of educational crisis, fueled in part by the publication of several reports critical of the quality of schools in the United States, makes the place of the arts even more precarious. With few exceptions, these reports have tended to downplay the significance of the arts for ensuring "educational excellence."[2] Instead, instruction in science, mathematics, and foreign language seems to be in the forefront of contemporary attempts at educational reform. Fourth, this trend is reinforced by a concern with what are thought to be educational "basics"—usually defined in terms of technical, quantifiable, and vocationally oriented skills, by means of which teachers may be held accountable, usually in terms of students' standardized test scores. Existing within a climate where quantification and "objective" tendencies are often paramount, the arts—presumably giving voice to the subjective, emotive, and noncognitive in human experience—may be too casually dismissed as ephemeral and of marginal value for educational achievement.

What these tendencies point to is the need for general classroom teachers to become more sensitive to the possibilities of aesthetic experience in their classrooms. Those of us concerned with the preparation of teachers have an especially important role to play in this regard. If we can help our students understand the value of aesthetic experience for themselves and their future pupils, we may help ensure the viability of the arts within public school classrooms. Moreover, if we can demonstrate to professional teachers how the arts may contribute significantly to their classroom activities, we will have performed an important service in defense of art and aesthetic education. These topics provide the focus for the present essay.

Building upon recent literature in curriculum theory, teacher preparation, and the philosophy of education, this chapter provides a theoretical basis, conceived in particular, foundational terms, for incorporating aesthetic experience into general teacher education programs.[3] In the next section, a summary of key points from the critically oriented research tradition in education will be provided. That tradition provides insight into the foundationally oriented teacher education program around which this effort to enlarge students' and teachers' aesthetic and political awareness is framed. The essential argument here is that since both school practices and teacher education programs necessarily embody political, moral, and ideological commitments, programs which prepare future teachers must assist students in furthering their understanding of these commitments and possible responses to them. The final section will outline the ways in which aesthetic value may play an important role in furthering this enlarged understanding for those involved in teaching. By discussing a specific teacher education program with which I have been involved, one that took a critical-foundational approach and incorporated aesthetic forms as a key element of it, we may be able to see more clearly how the arts may become rejuvenated and appropriately valued in schools.

The analysis of aesthetic experience and teacher education offered here will center on the linkages among school practice, reflective teacher preparation, and the dominance of larger social patterns and values. It is not permissible, in my view, for prospective teachers to be removed from such issues through the dominance of technical-rational, ameliorative programs of teacher preparation. Consistent with the discussions in chapters 4 and 5, I will demonstrate how aesthetic meanings not only may become reestablished in schools, but can help work toward larger social and personal transformations.

Critical Inquiry and Teacher Preparation

Attempts to situate school practices within a larger social context that illuminates their political significance have become more numerous and persuasive in the recent past, as noted in previous sections of this book. This larger context forms the backdrop for the current attempt to understand the work of teachers, the possibilities for teacher preparation, and the value of aesthetic experience within schools. Whatever we may think of the consequences—educational or political—that purportedly follow from that larger social context, attempts to understand schools as "encapsulated" institutions will not withstand scrutiny in the face of this critical tradition.[4]

There is sufficient argument and evidence to support the view that the particulars of school practice and questions of social control, ideological domination and resistance, and cultural reproduction must be seen as conjoined. As institutions that maintain our social identity even across times of apparent reform, schools reinforce a number of important political sensibilities, economic realities, and cultural practices. Based at least in part on an ethos of inequality, domination, and division, our social system requires institutions that not only maintain those disparities, but legitimate and safeguard them as well. That the process of ideological legitimation is served by one of our central institutions, the public school, is now beyond sensible contention.[5]

Since the formal and informal curriculum, evaluative practices, and pedagogy of schools serve to promote such ideological patterns, it is important for us as ethical and committed educators to respond to this situation.[6] Yet one of the continuing problems confronting critical theorists is precisely the question of which alternative set of possibilities we ought to support and work toward; the educational and political actions that we should undertake tend to be somewhat submerged in our critiques. Critical inquiry has largely been propelled by a desire to uncover relationships that were formerly hidden by the dominant traditions in social and educational theory. One of these, outlined in chapter 3, involves the relations between behavioral regularities in classrooms, especially concerning hierarchical forms of control, and the control of the nature and pace of work in factories. The telling metaphor here is the notion of "uncovering," an unearthing of something previously sealed. Along with this metaphor have come such notions as demystification, deconstruction, and the identification of false consciousness. The argument is that certain connections, structures, and overlapping commonalities have been covered over, for essentially ideological reasons, and that inquiry can now lay them bare. The process of uncovering these previously concealed connections has, however, focused on a critical reanalysis of existing practices, with relatively less attention paid to the articulation of productive possibilities that would move us beyond those practices.

I do not mean this so much as a criticism of the critical tradition in educational studies but as a description of what we must regard as its initial phases. Yet clearly the lack of productive possibility that would take us beyond critique has had its deleterious consequences. What is especially important to develop, at this point in the evolution of critical inquiry in education, is a more complete understanding of the contexts within which ideology operates, the localized microdomains that might be accessible to efforts at change, and the specific ways in which politically progressive actions may be fostered and commenced. Those understandings need to be linked, as well, with an emphasis on developing activities and practices that will reverse the tendencies toward social reproduction, estrangement, and acculturation in schools. One important context within which such actions offer the hope of change is on our work with undergraduate students who, as prospective teachers, will one day assume positions within institutions that might well be engaged in helping maintain current inequalities and forms of legitimation.

For purposes of analysis, we may usefully divide programs of teacher preparation into two broad categories: (1) those that take a technical-vocational or assimilationist approach, with a focus on "training" and (2) those that provide a more foundational orientation that focuses on educational studies.[7] While these are ideal types and may not represent actually operating programs, this characterization is valuable for heuristic purposes. Within technically oriented programs, there is a tendency to assume a taken-for-granted posture with respect to both current school practices and educational programs that serve to train people to replicate, more or less, dominant practices and roles. The work of preservice teachers is often limited to replicating current practice or modifying such practice within certain proscribed limits, with the result that teaching is seen as problematic only within a technical and ameliorative perspective. The aim of such teacher training efforts is often said to involve acquainting students with current practice (and perhaps increasing their proficiency at such practice), providing necessary survival skills to those entering the profession or easing the transition into preestablished roles.[8] As a consequence, activities and solutions to problems tend to be circumscribed by what we might call an "internal" perspective on teaching and schooling. The corollary of this tendency in teacher preparation programs is an emphasis on methods courses focusing on the specific skills, techniques, and forms of control deemed necessary for professional success. In this way the domain of teacher education is defined by and limited to extant classroom phenomena and processes, abstracted from wider, more encompassing social contexts. Teacher training programs that incorporate this vocational approach are sometimes regarded as apolitical and nonideological in their commitments and practices and as dominated instead by such seemingly neutral, professional concerns as increasing student achievement, maintaining discipline and order in the classroom, or providing, more generally, "meaningful experiences" to pupils. Within this approach to teacher preparation, normative questions such as those involving the values, ideas, and commitments that ought to guide teaching, the appropriate aims of education, and inquiry into the structures and contexts of schools are regarded as inappropriate or irrelevant. Perhaps the clearest statement of this point of view can be found in the admonition that, "the preservice student should not be exposed to theories and practices derived from ideologies and philosophies about the way schools should be. The rule should be to teach, and to teach thoroughly, the knowledge and skills that equip beginning teachers to work successfully in today's classroom."[9] The focus is here on preserving the educational status quo, regardless of the particular qualities being preserved, by focusing on current practice as determinant of educational decision making. Critical analysis and dialogue seem all but ruled out in such programs.

Moreover, given the commitment to preserving current forms of teaching, these programs promote "utilitarian teaching perspectives."[10] Students tend to accept the school practices they observe as forming the educational boundaries beyond which one may not trespass. Since the isolated classroom provides the basis for all important decision making, students tend to adopt an attitude of "excessive realism."[11] Analysis, theoretical inquiry, and critical dialogue that cannot be put to more or less immediate pragmatic use in classrooms are viewed with some skepticism. Given the increased number of hours that students must commonly spend in field settings (both prior to and during student teaching), programs which embody this technical-vocational orientation are even more likely to promote such points of view.[12]

The second orientation to teacher preparation, what I have referred to as a foundational approach, has a rather different, and to some extent contradictory, set of commitments. Instead of seeing educational foundations as composed of particular subjects, or specific courses, we should note that the foundations highlight a commonality of purposes, aims, or ways of thinking. This approach can be initially characterized by a commitment to open-ended inquiry, challenge, and critical interrogation. People engaged in teaching the foundations of education can be identified by a spirit of intellectual investigation and exchange, a commitment to understanding the roots of specific issues or questions, and a firm resolve to consider or help construct alternative possibilities. Used in this sense, the foundational areas in education may be understood as fostering a spirit of intellectual inquiry that has at least one foot in Platonic thought: to question, in gadfly fashion, the accepted wisdom in all areas of human investigation, to inquire into problems and ideas at their base, and to follow well-turned arguments and analyses in whatever direction they might lead. More specifically, this means that foundations proponents undertake analyses of the roots of educational issues, challenging conventional explanations, received opinions, and commonsensical ideas as these occur within educational discourse and public school classrooms. A part of this spirit of inquiry, this intellectual wrestling with established ways of seeing and understanding, involves a concern for those linkages between educational theory and practice, on the one hand, and broader social and ideological issues on the other. That is, those concerned with the foundations of education both recognize the political dynamics of schooling and characteristically undertake to raise issues about the nature of those dynamics. The foundations do not begin by assuming that a particular system of education—a commitment to the "basics" movement, say, in schools, or the current trend toward requiring standards-based teacher education programs is "natural," inevitable, or self-evident.[13] Yet this is precisely what those who take a vocational approach to teacher preparation tacitly or overtly do assume, in virtue of their programmatic emphases, or because of a lack of commitment to thorough inquiry. In short, foundational approaches to teacher preparation raise precisely those normative and ideological questions that more vocationally oriented programs have sought to sidestep.

As Crittenden has pointed out, the question of how teachers should be educated cannot be answered apart from taking a stand either explicitly or implicitly on how much of the existing institutional form and of the social context of schooling should be taken as given.[14] Berlak and Berlak put the essentially political nature of teacher preparation programs in this way: "All schooling, whatever the content or organization, however fragmented or unified it may be, including all programs for educating teachers is political. It is political in that it either encourages or does not encourage persons to develop and use their critical capacities to examine the prevailing political, social, and cultural arrangements and the part their own acts (as teachers or non-teachers) play in sustaining or changing these arrangements. If the curriculum and faculty of teacher education programs or courses fail to encourage critical inquiry into everyday problems of teaching and learning, a de facto political position has been taken."[15]

The technical—vocational approach to teacher preparation needs, finally, to be rejected on two grounds. In the first place, through the development of utilitarian teaching perspectives, the provision of survival skills, and the tendency for excessive realism to infiltrate students' perceptions when involved in such a vocationalized program, current situations become accepted as the educational given and thus unchallengeable. Current teaching practices become accepted as embodying the teaching domain, to be accommodated and adjusted to rather than critiqued, revised, or restructured. Such a process of uncritical acceptance would be indefensible even if we were able to develop criteria for teaching excellence of the sort that ultimately may be unspecifiable. In an important way, such a process of unthinking replication is, in Dewey's sense, miseducative, since it limits possibilities for further growth.[16] Second, many of the commonsense assumptions about the school's curriculum, pedagogical practices, evaluation tendencies, and so on, come to us already ideologically filtered, as we have seen in earlier chapters. While a common presumption is that schools are culturally fair, meritocratically organized, and politically neutral institutions, there is a substantial body of analysis and argumentation that indicates such a picture is not as accurate as we have assumed as a society (see chapter 3). Thus, to accept current school practice as given, to be acquiesced to by students engaged in a program of vocational training, is to run the risk of furthering the ideological nature of many school practices and their social consequences. Therefore, on both educative and political grounds, a foundational perspective must provide the basis for programs that prepare future teachers. The question which remains to be addressed is how aesthetic experience may be valuable within this foundational perspective for teacher preparation, valuable in a way that both helps ensure the viability of the arts in schools and works toward larger patterns of social transformation.

Aesthetic Value and Social Commitment

The social consequences of uncritically replicating current school policies and practices are untenable and must be tempered by the development of a foundationally oriented program of teacher preparation that embraces a range of inquiry-oriented issues and topics while focusing on new ways of thinking about schools, curriculum, and teaching. Here I provide the outlines of an aesthetic theory that has been useful in working toward such a foundational perspective, and I provide examples of how the foundational approach outlined above and the aesthetic theory sketched here have worked together in an actual teacher education program.[17]

In part because "art" names a species of things that have been so removed from other life events, it is primarily people and groups with appreciable wealth, status, and leisure that dominate the museum and concert hall. Because art has typically been regarded as removed from other life choices and possibilities and as the almost exclusive province of the privileged, it has lost an important measure of its social significance.[18] Though it may be said that the works of Mozart, Rembrandt, or Goethe represent humankind's greatest accomplishments, the ties between these accomplishments and the problems of living in contemporary society seem all but indiscernible.[19] We have to a significant extent lost a clear view of the power of aesthetic forms. There are several key factors involved in enhancing aesthetic meanings so that their potential for human life, generally, and for social change, specifically, can be understood by students and teachers.

First, as representational artifacts, works of art capture ideas, perspectives, and insights into human existence, thoughts that may not be possible through the use of other symbol systems.[20] The art object presents to the viewer an image of some reality that may not be expressible through other sorts of representations. The poet may speak of the mysteries, complexities, and uncertainties of life because he or she uses imagery, metaphor, and stylistic devices that go beyond more didactic, conventional, or stylized forms of language. Yet such uses of poetic language convey more than a different formal structure. They give voice to ideas, values, and perspectives that have a particular content or meaning. Moreover, our aesthetic encounters may bring to light alternative ways of seeing ourselves, others, and our position in the world. Consider, for example, the poetry and music of Bruce Springsteen.[21] The following lyrics appear in a contemporary work, "Used Cars":

My little sister's in the front seat with an ice cream cone
My ma's in the backseat sittin' all alone
As my pa steers her slow out of the lot for a
test drive down Michigan Avenue

Now my ma she fingers her wedding band
And watches the salesman stare at my old man's hands
He's tellin' us all 'bout the break he'd give us if he could but he just can't
Well if I could I swear I know just what I'd do . . .

Now mister the day the lottery I win I ain't ever
Gonna ride in no used car again . . .
My dad he sweats the same job from mornin' to morn
Me I walk home on the same dirty streets where I was born
Up the block I can hear my little sister in the front seat blowin' that horn
The sounds echoin' all down Michigan Avenue
Now mister the day my number comes in I ain't
Ever gonna ride in no used car again.[22]

In this song, insight is provided into the daily consequences of living in an environment where prestige, wealth, and influence are absent. In detailing a "slice of life" of such a family—the purchase of a "new used car—the author illuminates this situation in a way which captures an important material consequence of these social and economic facts. By utilizing the images of used cars, the weathered hands of someone who must work in the same low-paying job, a wedding ring, the lottery, and so on, Springsteen is able to poetically capture aspects of a particular cultural environment in a way that is not available to other forms of narrative or didactic accounts. In helping us see the personal, "up close" consequences of this environment in ways that may not be immediately obvious, this song tells us something about the world of this family and the larger social world as well. More globally, aesthetic experience may provoke for appreciators meanings that not only are pleasant, beautiful, or formally interesting, but that deepen our ability to experience and participate in the events of our, and others', lives. We might say that by contributing to our conscious understanding of the human and social world, the arts have a generalized cognitive capability.

Second, the insights which aesthetic experiences provide may make possible alternative ways of seeing, valuing, and making sense of our own situations and predicaments. While the ability of works of art to develop alternative perceptions and insights can be partly seen in their capacity to deepen our participation in social events, they do something that goes beyond such deepened participation as well. In providing perspectives that result in our seeing things in a new or different way, works of art help develop alternative worldviews that change what we see and value and virtually provide us with new, previously unseen "worlds." There are several ways that this creation of divergent worlds can happen: Aesthetic experiences may result in our seeing connections among things not normally united—e.g., through the use of metaphor. Or, in creating an image of what might be, works of art can provide a framework for alternative possibilities and divergent worlds. Again, in exposing something heretofore hidden, they may shape our reactions or responses to newly emerged worlds around us. The point here is that, at least on occasion, a work of art not only may deepen our insight into existing situations of which we are already more or less aware, but may create formerly undisclosed worlds in which to act.

Third, in presenting us with alternative perspectives and divergent worlds, aesthetic experiences at least tacitly challenge existing relationships, social patterns, and personal values. That is, not only can works of art offer us new possibilities, but they frequently challenge existing ones as well. Now often in practice the challenge posited by aesthetic experience will occur simultaneously with the presentation of alternative realities, the images of possibility implying a critique of current reality. Yet to realize fully the critical point of a work of art, we need to place the vision it offers alongside accepted patterns and perspectives. To do so requires that we break away from the decontextualized, abstracted view of aesthetic experience articulated in modern aesthetic theory. That is to say, in order for art to provide critical commentary, it must be seen as occupying space within the more typical day-to-day, sociohistorical context of actions and events.[23]

Fourth, it is essential that this revised picture of the aesthetic allow the arts to manifest their moral and political force within the lives of their audience. To see aesthetic experience as offering tacit moral guides based on a depiction of possibilities or critiques otherwise unrealized is not to reduce art to a vulgar instrumentality. Indeed, if art is to be more than a divorced, purified, and distinctly nonhuman enterprise, it must not rest on the notion that to truly appreciate art is to abstract it from other contexts. The construction of art objects is itself a generic, materially productive process that occurs within the interplay of human events, values, and decisions, a context wherein moral and political matters are not seen narrowly, but seen as central to human life. It is in taking a place in this center that aesthetic experience may become a vital, living force.

Aesthetic Meanings and Teacher Preparation That Is Foundational

The threads of the preceding analysis can be pulled together to illustrate how aesthetic experience can be an important part of teacher preparation programs based on foundational understandings. Though this approach has been outlined at a theoretical level exclusively, examples of how it has been implemented in a program of elementary teacher education will be discussed in this section. I focus on two of the principles that form the conceptual base for this program, illustrate for each the theoretical and practical aspects involved, and show how aesthetic experience plays a key role in their application.[24]

Principle one: we must recognize that knowledge and the institutions responsible for its dissemination are socially constructed and represent only one possibility among many. A substantial part of this idea involves recognizing the sociohistorical context of schooling and the forms of knowledge that are given legitimacy within it. What an analysis of this context reveals, again, is that schools were created in substantial part to serve as a vehicle for social control within a society that was facing the pressures of an industrialized, capitalistic, increasingly urbanized nation whose numbers were swelling, partly due to notable increases in immigration. Schools were not as dedicated to the ideals of equality of opportunity, the development of students' individual capacities, or the pursuit of academic excellence as many people have supposed.[25] To the extent that students realize that schools have historically served as a social safety valve and as a mechanism for reproducing social, cultural, and economic inequality, they begin to question basic assumptions about what is "given" within the world of schooling. Instead of taking for granted the school's organizational patterns, forms of knowledge, curricular ideologies, and so on, students are encouraged to see these as problematic and variable.

A central part of such inquiry involves students doing an abbreviated research study in a local classroom. Using an ethnographic approach to understanding education, students are aided in seeing beneath the surface reality, the educational given, of school experience. For example, students are asked to consider school life not from the view of teachers or administrators, but from the perspective of those "on the bottom," that is, the students—especially those who have been identified as "different" or "troublesome." Thus pupils who are frequently excluded from positive attention (those from racial and ethnic minority backgrounds, those who are habitually in some sort of difficulty regarding institutional expectations, or those who tend to become lost in the routinized grayness of institutional life) become a focus of concern for those undergraduate students contemplating a career in teaching.

A similar perspective is taken with respect to curriculum inquiry. One course attempts to deal with curriculum theory from historical and critical points of view. The development and popularity of various approaches to curriculum is situated within the social trends and political forces that were important during our society's history. An underlying motive of such inquiry is to take seriously the ideological and ethical question, Who benefits from the way curriculum theory and teaching has been understood historically? In addition, this course focuses on the concept of school knowledge itself: whose knowledge becomes accepted as appropriate curriculum content, how curriculum form is tied to technical controls in the workplace, and the like. Once again, the question of who benefits looms large throughout this approach to curriculum. Importantly, such questions are tied to the concrete workings of schools.

The involvement in critical inquiry and field research as a part of unpacking the meaning of the above principle goes some way toward redirecting the tendencies of utilitarian teaching perspectives, excessive realism, and uncritical replication common in vocational-technical approaches to teacher preparation. By emphasizing the socially constructed nature of schooling and the forms of knowledge that dominate it, students are aided in critically examining those foundational questions that compose the approach to teacher preparation being advocated. Moreover, this examination serves as a vehicle to question the very ideology of schooling that is usually fostered by vocationally oriented approaches to teacher preparation, increasing its educative and political salience.

Within this principle, the role of aesthetic experience can be seen in at least two ways. Attempts are made to recognize and value the ways in which aesthetic knowledge may be an important counter to the overly technicized, linear-based, efficiency-oriented activities that have dominated curriculum work.[26] The dominant model for curriculum making, based on the view that the goals for the curriculum are to be located in the current demands of the larger society and expressed in systematic, behaviorally oriented, and prespecified forms, has generated that factory model of curriculum making which is represented in teacher-proof instructional systems. While artistic production may not be as ungoverned or anarchistic as romanticized interpretations would have us believe, the kind of prespecification, systemization, and mechanization involved in much curriculum work seems incompatible with aesthetically sensitized experience.

At a more concrete level, efforts to incorporate aesthetic understandings into this first principle can be seen in two specific course offerings. First, such efforts have clear conceptual affinities with the teaching of reading and the language arts, even though these subjects are often among the most highly routinized and technicized areas of the public school curriculum. To counter these tendencies, the approach taken to the language arts is to regard these as part of a more generalized artistic/aesthetic domain. One of the questions asked, thus, is what reading would look like if it were an aesthetic activity, linked to other forms of aesthetic expression like movement, the visual arts, poetry, and so on. Students are involved in curriculum projects that incorporate this perspective and in the process help alter the more usual, systems-management approach to reading (with its elaborate instructional systems, skill sheets, "ability" grouping, emphasis on factual questioning, and the like). In this way aesthetic experience becomes one means of questioning the commonsensical in curriculum work, at the same time that more generalized cultural tendencies, such as an overreliance on linear thinking, quantification, process/product reasoning, and so on, are questioned. And since such characteristic ways of thinking and feeling are connected to the continuance of social, political, and economic configurations in their present form, the use of aesthetic experience as an alternative to more conventional curricular approaches may serve as one element in the movement toward larger social and cultural transformation.

At the heart of my criticism of technical-vocational approaches to teacher preparation is the tendency to assume that the way things are in education is the way they must or should be. In so doing, what we regard as commonsensical, taken for granted, or settled is in continual danger of becoming reified for ourselves and our students. Yet notice what an exploration of aesthetic forms does. Unhindered by the demands and constraints imposed by more routinized educational actions, able to engage constructively those imaginative and creative powers that schools tend to undervalue, the aesthetic becomes vitally useful in questioning the status quo of school practices. For example, it serves to critique the dominant models and metaphors of curriculum making, models that have historically dominated the field. To the extent that aesthetic meanings encourage such critical frames of reference in educational institutions, their more general capacity to help develop alternative ways of thinking and seeing is assisted, as is their ability to challenge conventional definitions and presuppositions.

Principle two: we must recognize the importance of developing alternative approaches to teaching, around which transformative theories and activities may be built. The enactment of this principle follows from and extends the process of critical reflection as already discussed and involves essentially three phases in the teacher preparation process. After becoming acquainted with the historically dominant approaches to curriculum work, students construct their own approach to curriculum and teaching, incorporating whatever ideas, values, and perspectives they find fitting. More concretely, students create their own curriculum project, which centers on some idea, issue, or subject area in which they have an interest. This project is intended to solidify previously articulated views of curriculum and pedagogy. The third phase in this process is the student teaching experience, which provides a forum for the exploration of teaching and curricular ideas that have been elaborated at a theoretical level and for the further sharpening of students' critical and reflective abilities. Consider two specific examples of how aesthetic experience has been effective in helping construct such alternatives.

One of the requirements for student teachers is to generate with their pupils an aesthetic project that can be implemented in their classroom. One project involved students constructing puppets and writing and acting out a play. During the activities associated with this project, activities which were totally pupil-initiated and open-ended, students began to work together in a kind of collaborative, nondirected way that was uncharacteristic of work in that particular classroom. The results were both surprising and encouraging for the students and teachers. Among other things, they began to question the usual way of proceeding and to appreciate the development of activities that were viable alternatives to the norm. While many of the second graders involved were initially rather worried about the parameters of the project ("Is this right?" "Is this what you want?" "Does mine have to be like Tommy's?" and the like were at first frequent questions asked of the student teacher), the activities once begun were exciting and empowering for them. The actual productions were a source of considerable pride and admiration for these children, as well as for their teachers. The excitement of the process and the satisfying results served to change one of the central reservations originally voiced by the staff, namely, that too much was being expected of this particular group of pupils.

Another project involved interweaving aesthetic activities, social issues, and political commitments specifically. This project dealt with different types of economic and political organizations, including capitalism, socialism, communism, and fascism. Many of the activities involved helping students understand the major concepts and values involved in such social forms, how they differed, and how to evaluate the pros and cons of each type. The culminating activity for this project involved students writing and directing a play in which these ideas were explored in concrete, understandable settings. In the process, political diversity became something more than a mere abstraction or theory. At the same time, students were able to challenge some of the usual preconceptions associated with discussions of this sort; these challenges were facilitated by the creative expression of the play in which they were actively involved. Such activities illustrate well how aesthetic sensitivity, ethical questioning, and political issues may become fused at the level of school practice, enhancing students' and teachers' ability not only to challenge the commonsensical, but also to help build alternative visions and futures.

The sometimes lavish praise accompanying support for the arts at a theoretical level does not always correspond to the facts of school life. While the reasons for this duplicity are complex, a good deal may be explained by reference to technical approaches to schooling and teacher preparation, approaches which reinforce the educational status quo, on the one hand, and to theories of aesthetic experience, theories which abstract it from more general human concerns, on the other. The foundational approach to teacher preparation outlined in this chapter, and the vision of aesthetic experience advocated throughout this book, may rejuvenate the arts in a way that promotes both educational and social change.

What the activities reported above illustrate is the possibility of politicizing aesthetic meanings so that they help challenge the "unquestionably" true, good, and proper. This does not entail reducing art to an instrumentally useful, propagandistic tool. Rather, unless we see the arts as being of liberating benefit to real people in actual lived situations and aesthetic education as related in some way to the larger social and ideological purposes that the school serves, we are apt to miss something important about the arts and their value for education.

The foundational approach sketched here seeks to unite progressive, scholarly oriented programs of teacher preparation with a strong, morally compelling vision of the aesthetic. In the end, we have no choice in our actions as researchers and educators: either we assist in the continuance of educational and social realities in their current forms, or we work toward other possibilities. It is in the ability of aesthetic experience to transform lived experience, the given of social interaction and meaning, and the facts of political consciousness that a revolutionized educational and social life may become possible. Working for fully aesthetic meanings, a more just and humane social order, and a foundational approach to educational inquiry and practice embodies a common sentiment.

Notes

1. Throughout this chapter, I will use the term "aesthetic experience" to mean our conscious, intentional interaction with, and appreciation of, works of art. Though, as discussed in chapter 1, aesthetic experiences are possible with natural, nonartifactual phenomena, I will limit this phrase to experiences with objects that are intended to be perceived as art. At the same time, I will continue to insist on a lack of separation between the "fine arts" and the "popular arts" in terms of their aesthetic value.

2. See, for example, the National Commission on Excellence in Education, *A Nation at Risk* (Washington, D.C.: U.S. Government Printing Office, 1983); John Goodlad, *A Place Called School* (New York: McGraw-Hill, 1984). For a report that cites the importance of the arts within liberal education, see Mortimer Adler, *The Paideia Proposal* (New York: Macmillan, 1982). Critiques of *A Nation at Risk* and *The Paideia Proposal* are found in *Curriculum Inquiry* 15, no. 1 (Spring 1985); respectively, these are, Landon E. Beyer, "The Political Roots of National Risk"; and Michael W. Apple, "Old Humanists and New Curricula: Politics and Culture in *The Paideia Proposal.*

3. While many programs may be labeled "foundational" in spirit or origin, I use this term to mean those programs that tend to question the taken-for-granted, assumed, and given of educational experience and that see school practice as a species of social and political action, subject to moral, ideological, and cultural debate. See Landon E. Beyer and Kenneth M. Zeichner, "Teacher Training and Educational Foundations: A Plea for Discontent," *Journal of Teacher Education* 33, no. 3 (May-June 1982).

4. Seymour B. Sarason, *The Culture of the School and the Problem of Change*, 2nd ed. (Boston: Allyn and Bacon, 1982).

5. This is not to imply, of course, that all the work within this theoretical tradition has been completed and we can now move on to something else, nor that everyone agrees on the particular analyses that have been conducted or their consequences for action. I do mean to suggest, though, that a decontextualized, abstracted view of educational institutions is no longer tenable.

6. On the formal curriculum and the relationship between the content of school knowledge and the larger ideological patterns, see, for example, Michael F. D. Young, ed., *Knowledge and Control* (London: Collier-Macmillan, 1971); Geoff Whitty and Michael F. D. Young, eds., *Explorations in the Politics of School Knowledge* (Nafferton, England: Nafferton Books, 1976); Michael W. Apple, *Ideology and the Curriculum* (Boston: Routledge & Kegan Paul, 1979); Walter Feinberg, *Understanding Education* (New York: Cambridge University Press, 1983); Michael W. Apple and Lois Weis, eds., *Ideology and Practice in Schooling* (Philadelphia: Temple University Press, 1983); and Jean Anyon, "Ideology

and U.S. History Textbooks," *Harvard Educational Review*, 49 (August 1979). On the informal curriculum, see Elizabeth Vallance, "Hiding the Hidden Curriculum: An Interpretation of the Language of Justification in Nineteenth-Century Educational Reform," in *Curriculum and Evaluation*, ed. Arno Bellack and Herbert M. Kliebard (Berkeley: McCutchan, 1977); Samuel Bowles and Herbert Gintis, *Schooling in Capitalist America* (New York: Basic Books, 1976); and Jean Anyon, "Social Class and the Hidden Curriculum of Work," *Journal of Education* 162 (Winter 1980). On evaluation practices, see Michael W. Apple and Landon E. Beyer, "Social Evaluation of Curriculum," *Educational Evaluation and Policy Analysis* 5, no. 4 (Winter 1983). For an indication of the uniformity of pedagogical practices over time and across geographical distances, see Jacob Riis, *The Children of the Poor* (New York: Charles Scribner's Sons, 1982); Kenneth Sirotnik, "What You See Is What You Get: Consistency, Persistency, and Mediocrity in Classrooms," *Harvard Educational Review* 53, no. 1 (February 1983); and Theodore R. Sizer, *Horace's Compromise: The Dilemma of the American High School* (Boston: Houghton Mifflin, 1984).

7. See Landon E. Beyer, Walter Feinberg, Jo Anne Pagano, and James Anthony Whitson, *Preparing Teachers as Professionals: The Role of Educational Studies and Other Liberal Disciplines* (New York: Teachers College Press, 1989).

8. For survival skills, see Lillian Katz, "Issues and Problems in Teacher Education," in *Teacher Education: Of the Teacher, by the Teacher, for the Child*, ed. Bernard Spodek (Washington, DC: National Association for the Education of Young Children, 1974). For transitions, see Frances Fuller, *Relevance for Teacher Education: A Teacher Concerns Model* (Austin: University of Texas Center for Teacher Education, 1971).

9. B. O. Smith, "On the Content of Teacher Education," in *Exploring Issues in Teacher Education: Questions for Future Research*, ed. E. Hall et al. (Austin: University of Texas R & D Center for Teacher Education, 1980), pp. 23–24.

10. Lawrence Iannaccone, "Student Teaching: A Transitional Stage in the Making of a Teacher," *Theory into Practice* 2, no. 2 (June 1983); and B. Robert Tabachnick et al., "Teacher Education and the Professional Perspectives of Student Teachers," *Interchange* 10, no. 4 (1980).

11. Katz, "Issues and Problems in Teacher Education."

12. Landon E. Beyer, "Field Experience, Ideology, and the Development of Critical Reflectivity," *Journal of Teacher Education* 35, no. 3 (May-June 1984).

13. For advocates of this movement, see Linda Darling-Hammond, Arthur E. Wise, and Stephen P. Klein, *A License to Teach: Building a Profession for* Twenty-First *Century Schools* (Boulder: Westview Press, 1995); National Commission on Teaching & America's Future, *What Matters Most: Teaching for America's Future* (New York: National Commission on Teaching & America's Future, 1996); and National Council for Accreditation of Teacher Education, *Program Standards for Elementary Teacher Preparation* (Washington, DC: National Council for Accreditation of Teacher Education, 1998). For a critique of that position, see Landon E. Beyer, "Teacher Education and the 'New Professionalism': The Case

of the USA," in *Tomorrow's Teachers: International and Critical Perspectives on Teacher Education*, ed. Alan Scott and John Freeman-Moir (Christchurch, New Zealand: Canterbury University, 2000).

14. Brian Crittenden, "Some Prior Questions in the Reform of Teacher Education," *Interchange* 4, nos. 2 and 3 (1973).

15. Harold Berlak and Ann Berlak, *Dilemmas of Schooling: Teaching and Social Change* (London: Methuen, 1981).

16. John Dewey, *Democracy and Education* (New York: Free Press, 1916).

17. The examples provided in this paper are taken from my experience in the elementary education program at Knox College, where I taught from 1981 to 1984, and again from 1988 to 1994. For further examples of the kind of foundational teacher practices that have been undertaken by former students, see Landon E. Beyer, *Creating Democratic Classrooms: The Struggle to Integrate Theory and Practice* (New York: Teachers College Press, 1996).

18. Raymond Williams, *Marxism and Literature* (Oxford: Oxford University Press, 1977).

19. Ibid.; see also Raymond Williams, *Problems in Materialism and Culture* (London: New Left Books, 1980); and Landon E. Beyer, "Philosophical Work, Practical Theorizing, and the Nature of Schooling," *Journal of Curriculum Theorizing* 5, no. 1 (Winter 1983).

20. Nelson Goodman, *Languages of Art* (New York: Bobbs Merrill, 1968).

21. I chose the work of Bruce Springsteen to illustrate this point for a couple of reasons. First, he represents in my view one of the best contemporary composers of popular music, and one of the tasks facing us is breaking down the barriers between "high" and "popular" art. Second, his music represents popular working-class art in contemporary U.S. society.

22. Bruce Springsteen, "Used Cars," on his album *Nebraska*, produced by SNY, 1990 recording number 7.

23. Williams, *Marxism and Literature*; and Williams, *Problems in Materialism and Culture*.

24. See Beyer, "Field Experience, Ideology, and the Development of Critical Reflectivity," for a more complete discussion of the principles mentioned here.

25. David Nasaw, *Schooled to Order: A Social History of Public Schooling in the United States* (New York: Oxford University Press, 1979); David Tyack, *The One Best System: A History of American Urban Education* (Cambridge: Harvard University Press, 1974); and Michael B. Katz, *Class, Bureaucracy, and Schools: The Illusion of Educational Change in America* (New York: Praeger, 1971).

26. Dwayne Huebner, "Curricular Language and Classroom Meanings," in *Curriculum Theorizing: The Reconceptualists*, ed. William F. Pinar (Berkeley: McCutchan, 1975); and Elliott Eisner, *The Educational Imagination* (New York: Macmillan, 1979).

Chapter 7

The Arts as Personal and Social Communication: Popular/Ethical Culture in Schools

May Sarton opens her moving autobiographical and social story, *Journal of a Solitude*, with these thoughts:

> BEGIN HERE. It is raining. I look out on the maple, where a few leaves have turned yellow, and listen to Punch, the parrot, talking to himself and to the rain ticking gently against the windows. I am here alone for the first time in weeks, to take up my "real" life again at last. That is what is strange—that friends, even passionate love, are not my real life unless there is time alone in which to explore and to discover what is happening or has happened. Without the interruptions, nourishing and maddening, this life would become arid. Yet I taste it fully only when I am alone here and the house and I resume old conversations.[1]

I find all of May Sarton's work engaging and revealing, not only in its poetic appeal, but simultaneously in its ability to disclose something of my own experiences, to flash a light on things that otherwise remain in the sometimes hidden recesses of my awareness. The passage just cited, for example, brings to mind the ineluctable tensions between solitude and solidarity in my own life, and the whole that they form. It recalls my own need to escape the network of demands, connections, tensions, and delights of social life, the need to revel in the solace of my own wilderness retreat which has been a real home for me, especially during those times that were tumultuous during the past twenty years. But Sarton's words are more than reminders of things I already know or sense: they help bring those things to life, providing new interpretations, ways of thinking, and unanticipated meanings. They expand my own experiences of togetherness and solitude.

A music album by Jerry Jeff Walker, *Hill Country Rain*, includes a song called "The Man He Used to Be." The song is about a man looking back, finding out how different things are now from the way they were, discovering how quickly and effortlessly his identity seems to have been transformed:

So that's where my head was at
Was in a book an' a funky hat
I was on the road with Kerouac,
Searching for the truth
An' sometimes I'm amazed,
Lookin' back at a certain phase
I wet my thumb and I turn the page
Of what was I tryin' to prove . . .

I shake my head an' I laugh
At a faded photograph
Of a total stranger starin' back at me—
There's no man stranger to himself
Than the way he used to be

There's a closet full of worn out boots,
Skeletons and three-piece suits,
A million hats and attitudes
An' very few regrets
And here I stand, faded jeans
An ol' T-shirt that don't say anything
And who knows what tomorrow brings,
Ah, it ain't over yet

And I just shake my head and I laugh
At a faded photograph
Of a total stranger
Starin' back at me
There's no man stranger to himself
There's no man stranger to himself
Than the man he used to be

Now some folks they get me confused
With someone else,
They once knew
I know the guy they're referrin' to—
He ain't been 'round for years;
An' I shake my head and I laugh
At the faded photograph
Of a total stranger staring back at me
An' I can see it in the eyes—
It was a whole other life

Of a total stranger
Starin' back at me
No, there's no man stranger to himself
There's no man stranger to himself
There's no man stranger to himself
Than the man he used to be. . . . [2]

Our identities, this song reminds us, are fluid, subject to imaginative reinterpretation, framed by other points of reference and experiences with the world. We may well look back on aspects of our own lives not only in wonder, but with incredulity. Still, to become someone different may be exactly to be ourselves, that is, the kind of being who partakes in both change and constancy.

Commonality and Difference

People are obviously different, in numerous and often important ways: age, gender, race, ethnicity, geographic origin and present location, language, social class, and sexual orientation. "Difference" and "otherness" have recently taken on a new primacy, perhaps constituting some of the defining elements of what it means to live in late twentieth century. An emphasis on difference sensitizes us to realities and traditions that have been largely submerged within dominant ideas, traditions, and modes of political and cultural power. The consequences of cultural homogenization have been noted by many and include (1) the manipulation by one or another dominant elite that claims universalizable standards that maintain their status; (2) claims that particular characteristics are normatively privileged, with the consequence that those not possessing them are deviant and marginalized; and (3) the quieting of resistance through the creation of patterns of allegedly universal discourse, patterns that delegitimate other forms articulated by nonpowerful groups. In the process of exposing the manipulative patterns that have developed through homogenization, difference itself appears to be valorized, ironically, as a transcendent good, or at least as a fact of postmodern life.[3]

Others continue to claim that there are realities that do in fact seem widely, if not universally, shared and defining of human life—for example, interactions in which emotions like anger, love, sorrow, or joy are prominent. Or maybe there are experiences that all human beings undergo at one time or another and that define a commonality transcending difference—birth, death, and struggle of various sorts being primary candidates. Such claims seek to document the ways in which people share certain traits or states, over and against the differences that place us in separate spheres.

Disputes about universality and difference primarily involve neither metaphysical abstractions nor analytic distinctions about which there are divergent perspectives. When people choose one side over the other in these disputes it does, I believe, make a difference in how they see themselves, their responsibility to others, their relation to physical and social worlds, and their sense of the future in which they might partake. At the same time, the sometimes shrill commentary among those with different starting points has not, I believe, served us well in terms of the creation of a genuinely democratic ethos, among other things.[4]

The divide separating those who steadfastly cling to commonality from those who want to stake a claim on behalf of difference cannot, in the end, be breached. We are, after all, both same and different, from each other and from ourselves at different times. Nothing quite stands still, severed from what has gone before and what will come after, or from other concurrent realities; yet not all is predictable. We recognize ourselves in the mirror and yet wonder how we came to look different than we used to, or at least different than we thought we did. One day we see the things that we may never share with a person and are stunned the next by a new connection that could not have been anticipated. We are able to note difference and divergence because we simultaneously perceive something shared, we recognize and appreciate what is common and in doing so value what is different—in others and ourselves. To be connected is to crave solitude; to see the person we used to be is to see ourselves as different and continuous.

The arts provide rich avenues for such realizations. Indeed, helping us come to know each other and ourselves as same and different and to see in and through this knowledge both current realities and future possibilities may be among the special virtues of the arts. As creations embodying symbolic domains that disclose something about the worlds in which we live and work as well as other, yet-to-be created worlds, the arts make possible moral imaginations that reach from what we now feel, think, and perceive to what may be possible and obligatory for the future. They make us aware of things only sensed on the periphery, shaping us and at the same time helping construct the worlds we know as same and different. They provoke forms of communication that, in changing us, change what we experience as same and different, and so provide glimpses of what is possible.

Experience and Expression

People have experiences, virtually as a condition of daily life, that include other people, places, objects, and locations. Indeed it might be said that life itself is impossible (or at least less valuable) if we don't experience certain things or events. Not all of our experiences have the same quality or significance, since they vary by intensity, relevance, novelty, meaningfulness, duration, and so on. Some experiences are relatively trivial or fleeting while others literally "stay with us" for a lifetime, becoming a part of who we are. A central part of the oppressiveness of certain situations—being jailed, living with narcissistic barriers, or being schooled in certain kinds of institutions—is that the range of experiences they permit is severely restricted or mindlessly repetitive.

Restrictions on experience, however, do not appear only because of external constraints. We often limit our own experiential possibilities. For "having an experience" is not synonymous with simply "living through a situation" or being physically present at a particular place and time as "events unfold." If we are oblivious to the circumstances that we are in, or perceive them as predictable, ordinary, and commonplace (and hence unremarkable), we may reasonably be said not to have had an experience of those circumstances. So one condition for having an experience seems to be a wide-awakeness with respect to our surroundings, our location within some phenomenal field, and our actions and their consequences.[5] To only be acted on within a physical setting, to be reduced to an object buffeted about by external forces that go unrecognized, is to fail to have an experience of that setting.[6]

Having an experience seems to require more than a bare awareness of external events and of our responsibility as actors in the world. For there is a rather large range of meanings that experiences provide to different people, and to the same person at different times, meanings that go beyond the unfolding of physical processes and our awareness of them. These divergent meanings may be created by a fund of previous experiences that a person has undergone, by reflections on those experiences that make similar ones more vivid or understandable, by conversations with others who have been in similar situations, or by suggestive ideas, points of view, or ways of seeing that urge us to interpret that experience differently. In short, some sort of mental activity accompanies mere physical occurrences as they become experiences. This mental activity can take a number of different forms and can at least sometimes change our view of that occurrence, or the physical world itself, and hence can help create new experiences. It may also change the way we see our actions in the world ourselves and as people actively engaged in creating and valuing experiences.

Consider a situation in which I have an appointment to keep, one that requires that I walk from point A to point B, and consider that the appointment is critically related to accomplishing something about which I care deeply. My mind is fixed on the events that will take place at point B, and I select a route to travel there that will ensure that I arrive promptly. My actual movements along the path I select, and the surroundings I pass by, only provide the context for accomplishing a valued end; they are not of themselves meaningful or even part of my conscious awareness. Given my concentration on things that are to come, and only the most narrow, utilitarian awareness of the actual path leading from A to B, I cannot be said to have experienced the environment that exists between those points. I have an experience of something during my walk between the two locations, perhaps rehearsing the points I wish to make in the conversation that is to take place, but I have not experienced the physical environment in which those mental activities took place.

Now suppose that I successfully conclude my activities at point B and retrace my steps. Since the activities for the sake of which I began my trip have been completed, I can now focus on other things, so that I become more open to the environment on my return trip. I now notice several things in the environment—trees, flowers, animals, the pattern and shape of clouds on the horizon, and so on—that before went unseen. I stop to look at the juxtaposition of colors formed by the leaves and bark of different tree species and the way the sunlight is reflected off a nearby rock formation. I have, in short, an experience of the environment of which I am now a part. I begin to appreciate the colors, shapes, patterns, smells, and sounds of the environment and frequently stop to consider their particular qualities and charms.

Suppose further that I return to that same location a month later and strike up a conversation with someone who is photographing aspects of the landscape and its flora and fauna. The photographer not only points out features of some things that I previously noticed, but makes comments about the ecology of the area, the connections among plant and animal species, and the ways in which they form a cohesive, mutually sustaining network of relationships. I see not only individual plants and animals, appreciating their aesthetic or botanical/biological qualities, but the interconnections among the elements of the environment. My experience has been enhanced not because something physically new has been added to the environment, but because of a change in my understanding and level of awareness. In making connections among objects and becoming more discriminate in my observations, I see new things and see other things differently. In short, I have a different experience, and hence live in a new world.

My interests may become more expansive. I may become so engaged with the wonders of the natural world that I undertake a program of ecological study. I read a number of articles and books dealing with topics and issues related to the environment, attend seminars, and go to meetings of the local chapter of Greenpeace. Eventually I come to appreciate both the subtleties of ecosystems and the threats to them posed by what many people think of as progress. Such study may incite me not only to appreciate and spend more time in an environment that was before only instrumentally valued, but to become involved in efforts to protect the environment, and to actively resist the destruction of old-growth forests. I become, in short, a different person, capable of qualitatively different experiences and actions in the world.

The general point I want to emphasize through this illustration is that experiences become enriched, intensified, or more meaningful not simply through immersion in an environment but through a series of mental/intellectual/perceptual shifts. My experiences become deeper or more valuable because of changes I make (with the help of others, to be sure) and not simply by returning to the same environment again and again. In brief, mental activities and (broadly speaking) inquiry may allow us to have new experiences and/or to deepen otherwise tepid ones. This is not to say that physical circumstances are only a forum for the playing out of mental constructs, but to say that the latter may help reconstruct experience—that experience is both mental and physical.

If mental events help create experiences of physical objects and environments, it seems even more clear that mental states shape social experiences and possibilities. Consider the problems many people have relating to those who are "different" in terms of their level of functioning and who are, accordingly, labeled and placed in special institutions or classrooms. Many people feel awkward or even threatened by those who are autistic, for example. They make excuses for not being able to comfortably interact with them or find ways to avoid contact with them altogether. Such reactions may not be altered through forced exposure to people with autism—indeed, their discomfort may in fact only be heightened. Thus, simply arranging situations where people will be exposed to those who are different will not necessarily change their attitudes or actions in positive ways.[7] On the other hand, learning more about what autism is—its effects and characteristics as well as how to beneficially interact with autistic people—may change our preconceptions about such "different" people and may change the ways we are able to interact with them. Experiencing people with autistic traits with understanding and sensitivity—like experiencing the natural environment in increasingly engaging ways—may be enhanced by mental events as much as by physical proximity.[8]

At another level, reflections on our experiences are frequently inadequate in dealing with some troubling issue or personal crisis. There are a number of ways that we may try to deal with this situation: discussing it with friends, seeking advice from people with particular forms of expertise, engaging in psychotherapy, and so on. It is frequently possible for an "outsider," as it were, to uncover patterns of conduct or to develop insights into our lives, ones that we are incapable of providing on our own at a particular time. This testifies to the important fact that people not directly involved in experiences we have had are sometimes able to make better sense of them than we can, and they may help us deal with their consequences better than we are able to alone. The same thing is true, I would argue, of more social situations or problems. A level of understanding regarding the day-to-day dynamics and consequences of working- class life, for example, may be uniquely available to working-class people who have lived through them. We may, after all, gain something valuable about direct experience with class-based antagonisms and oppression, something that is not possible to appreciate without that experience. On the other hand, "classism" is more than a matter of direct experience. Just as experiencing a physical environment differently may depend on reflection and inquiry—in short, on what we normally call "theoretical work"—experiencing and understanding the dynamics of class are not exclusively the province of members of that class. Classism involves complex issues and conceptual understandings as well as forms of analysis, all of which are not available exclusively through direct experience of specific situations. The same is true for the dynamics of race and gender and other forms of oppression as well. It is a mistake to say that Clarence Thomas and Phyllis Schafly are able to provide insightful analyses of race and gender dynamics just because of the facts of their personal racial and gender identity.

The arts, like people situated differently in times of personal stress and difficulty, provide forums in which we can develop or enhance certain kinds of social experiences and create alternative realities. They provide one of the primary means by which human activity can be encapsulated, re-presented, disclosed, and symbolized. In helping us develop narratives that recreate experiences in and of the world, they provide avenues for insight and routes for personal and social action. Works of art embody forms of expression that can remake experience, as they provide means for unifying involvement and reflection, and allow us to gain perspective on commonality and difference.

This disclosure/remaking role of the arts reflects their status as both material and symbolic experience. An artwork depicting a particular landscape is not to be mistaken for a physical landscape through which we move. Nor is a novel like *Betsey Brown* an actual experience of living through the tumult of the late 1950s.[9] Yet to recognize this is not to conclude that the arts as symbolic creations exist separately from daily life and activity. Indeed, the "virtualness" of aesthetic forms does allow them a real, and important, separation from the ebb and flow not only of events, but of conventional wisdom, the commonsensical, and the accepted. The arts are related to daily experience yet not constituted through it; an appreciation of the arts creates spaces for reflection and action, helping our moral imaginations leap from what is to what might be, and at least sometimes helping reconstruct the worlds we inhabit. In this sense a work of art may well be more "real" than a physical occurrence, as it nudges us to possibilities unavailable within that occurrence itself. Moreover, such an artwork, in challenging our presuppositions and our usual reference points, may provide a more potent avenue for enlivened experience and social change.

The Arts as Communication

To communicate is to formulate and express ideas, feelings, states of mind, points of view, etc., via symbolic universes that we come to share with others. Novels, films, songs, paintings, and the other forms of art contain elements that, together with a responsive perceiver, generate meanings without preconceived limits. It is the special province of the arts to create imaginative possibilities that lead us out into the world at the same time that they help us understand ourselves and assist in creating who we are and whom we are to become (which are themselves aspects of difference and sameness).

These possibilities of art as communication and of art forms that communicate across difference offer only a potential for aesthetic endeavors, of course. This potential may be enhanced via the creation of critical aesthetic theories such as those developed in chapters 2 and 4, theories that help us decipher aesthetic experience and allow it to become a force for action in the world. Aesthetic experience, like all other kinds, contains both sensory inputs and intellectual ability. Any cultural politics must allow for the sort of aesthetic experience that is tied to social and cultural transformation. This presumes some commonality of purpose—within the interconnectedness of sameness and difference—both among the arts as a force for redirection of experience and among people engaged in building worlds collectively. These presumptions can be seen as undermining the view that difference is of singular importance.

Though the arts have been widely prized for their ability to affect the emotions and perceptions of individuals during the time they spend with them, their creative potential is stunted if they are limited to that domain. Indeed, one problem in saying that the arts constitute a particular fund of experiences—even if we can decide the complex issue of what the aesthetic elements are that create them[10]—is that such an approach, if left unexamined and disconnected, can come to constitute an individualistic, essentially psychologized domain. Left out is a consideration of the social/structural pressures that shape and reshape individual experience. An awareness and critical understanding of such pressures is essential if we are to develop a critical aesthetic that carries with it the possibilities of social change. Recall the ideas of Barry and Flitterman-Lewis when they state that "every act (eating an orange, building a table, reading a book) is a social act; the fundamentally human is social. Theory enables us to recognize this and permits us to go beyond individual, personally liberating solutions to a 'socially' liberated situation."[11] This approach to feminist art forms moves us beyond the disinterestedness and ideological isolation that were dominant in modern aesthetic theory. It also provides clues about what may be central to such art beyond its being a part of collective "women's experience" and suggests ways in which different art forms might also be tied to collective struggles mandating some commonality. That is, there is no essentialist "women's experience" that can be neatly disconnected from other kinds of experience. Nor is it the case—to follow the line of argument running through this chapter—that women's experience (and the experience of others) is completely inaccessible to those lacking certain traits or histories. Perhaps most importantly, this understanding of feminist art pushes us to consider the need for a collective, integrated, cohesive response to women's oppression. In seeing the similarities as well as the differences among feminist and other art forms, alliances might well be formed in which common sources of social dislocation and oppression might be highlighted and points of contact might be created, ones that foster individual and collective liberation. These things require a reexamination of some of our deepest beliefs about the arts and their purposes.

In his criticism of the dominant traditions in aesthetic theory, Raymond Williams discusses the ways in which the arts of a period help construct a "structure of feeling" that gives shape to, and helps reveal, social processes, objects, relationships, and ways of life; this structure of feeling is in one sense "the culture of a period: it is the particular living result of all the elements in the general organization. And it is in this respect that the arts of a period . . . are of major importance." In the arts, "in the only examples we have of recorded communication that outlives its bearers, the actual living sense, the deep community that makes the communication possible, is naturally drawn upon."[12] The arts not only require a community in order to be understood as a kind of communication, but foster the development of such communities as well as help chart directions for them.

A materialist, progressive theory of aesthetics gives voice to aesthetic value, political possibility, and personal liberation and points as well to the ways and the arenas within which such a perspective is practically feasible. Two propositions are especially important here. First, in communicating images, ideas, situations, or themes, all art contains at least implicit ways of seeing, constructing, and making sense of the world, of communicating a vision of what life is or could become. It at once hides and discloses political and social visions. Such visions may be harder or easier to discern, given a particular work's complexity, its use of symbolic forms, and the extent to which the members of the audience share symbolic and experiential reference points and are open to aesthetic forms that challenge conventional ways of seeing. Second, while aesthetic experiences are always personal in some significant sense, they are social as well. Not only do they require a familiarity with shared symbolic universes, but their meaning cannot be limited to an individuated, face-to-face encounter. If the arts are to be a force for emancipation, we must recognize that no genuine liberation movement can be totally or exclusively individuated or psychological, as important as these elements frequently are. "The social" and "the personal" cannot be conceived as separable, reified categories, each representing forms of autonomous existence. Yet the political import of art must be felt by and acted on by individuals. If "art" and "politics" cannot be isolated, neither can "personal" and "social" change which the arts can help forge.

The sort of critical aesthetic theory that is consistent with an integration of the personal with the political, commonality with difference, and culture with politics sees the arts as connected to structural and personal relations that are complex, dynamic, and sometimes oppositional. By locating social experience within this complex set of constructs, and by seeing the arts as a basis for both understanding and transforming the socially constructed definitions of the social, art, and politics, a critical aesthetic practice that can help alter our consciousness, our schools, and our social situations may be realized.

As a project with socially transformative possibilities, the construction of a critical aesthetic education must be broad enough, and open enough, to foster expressions of difference while providing forums for the re-creation of experience, understood as the conjunction of physical and mental phenomena. This in turn may move us toward the generation of a community within which diversity and points of intersection are equally important constitutive elements. In general we might say that the kind of community that may really work toward personal and social reconstruction is one in which difference and commonality cohabit, and where aesthetic experience can become one vital path toward experiences, understandings, and actions.

Critical and Progressive Possibilities for Aesthetic Education

Young people grow up within an array of cultural, ideological, and social realities. Through a variety of socialization influences, they develop understandings of the world in which they live and learn to participate in that world in various ways. A major influence on these understandings comes from the messages contained in forms of popular culture transmitted through television, music, film, video productions (games and movies), magazines, and so on. These messages often conflict with the very values and practices required for the development of a critical aesthetic. Children and adolescents are continually bombarded by ideologically embedded messages about what is normal, necessary, or appropriate: the images of women in newspapers and magazines and a variety of other media; the requirements for masculinity and femininity in children's stories and novels; the violence depicted on television (as well as the violence witnessed by many children every day in the school playground and many neighborhoods); the racism in open view in many families, neighborhoods, and communities; and the systemic nature of the oppression visited on the poor, people of color, and women. These forms of consciousness assist in developing and shaping students' perceptions, attitudes, and interests and help make them who they are. They often lead to strongly held interests and commitments in our students. And in some ways such interests represent the kinds of realities that child-centered progressives have thought should be central to the creation of the school curriculum. Yet it is these very interests that often encode sentiments and priorities that are the very antithesis of what is required for significant individual reexamination and social change.

Pretending that the socially constructed beliefs that students bring to schools are inconsequential results in superficial forms of student participation and morally and politically insignificant educational experiences. They may learn to disengage "private" values and perspectives from the "official/public" world of schools. As a result, ideas and issues prompted by classroom experience may remain disconnected from the students' actual perceptions and predilections that affect the meaning and significance of school and social life. Even when students listen attentively to teachers' and texts' discussions of the horrors and injustices of racism, for example, their understanding will be only superficial or rhetorical if we do not help them make connections between their own experiences and beliefs and the possibilities for equality, if we do not help them re-envision their experience. This is a fundamental problem associated with the use of conventional textbooks and other sanitized and dislocated forms of knowledge and curricula.

Beyond the necessity of dealing squarely with current social realities and getting below the surface of forms of conventional wisdom, educators need to help students imagine new possibilities and then find ways to work toward creating them. It should not be surprising that many politicians, businesspeople, and educators fail to take seriously the need to revive the imagination of our children and young people. Whether immersed in a narrow or vulgar pragmatism, focused on the near term, or determined to hide the "underside" of American society, the retreat from visionary possibilities, and even speculations, provides one source of numbing continuity and social stasis. As Maxine Greene so eloquently reminds us, it is the imaginative powers of people that need especially to be cherished and released:

> Not always but oftentimes, the extent to which we grasp another's world depends on our existing ability to make poetic use of our imagination, to bring into being the "as if" worlds created by writers, painters, sculptors, filmmakers, choreographers, and composers, and to be in some manner a participant in artists' worlds

> reaching far back and ahead in time. . . . For me as for many others, the arts provide new perspectives on the lived world. As I view and feel them, informed encounters with works of art often lead to a startling defamiliarization of the ordinary. . . . What I have habitually taken for granted . . . frequently reveals itself in unexpected ways because of a play I have seen, a painting I have looked at, a woodwind quintet I have heard. And now and then, when I am in the presence of a work from the border, let us say, from a place outside the reach of my experience until I came in contact with the work, I am plunged into all kinds of reconceiving and revisualizing. I find myself moving from discovery to discovery; I find myself revising, and now and then renewing, the terms of my life.[13]

I argued earlier that the arts provide a perhaps exemplary route for re-envisioning experience. If this is the case, the problem of only pseudo-commitments being developed in schools because of the disengagement of social life from school experience may be countered by the incorporation of forms of popular culture into the curriculum. That disengagement may be overcome by the arts in two ways. First, by encouraging and helping to provide to students the intellectual means by which they can critically analyze the forms of art that are important to them, students can in turn "read" the important aesthetic and social messages that the arts often communicate. Both productive and corruptive readings, of course, are available to our students. Second, by engaging in imaginative visions and imaginative renderings of the aesthetic, artists and teachers can help students see beyond the conventional and the mundane and look toward a future more aesthetically uplifting and morally respectable. Recognizing the educational significance of the arts, especially popular culture (for good or ill), we underscore the potency of the aesthetic for day-to-day life, acknowledging, as outlined in the previous section, its potential as a form of communication. We also see firsthand the real affects that images can have on students' consciousness and actions. But merely acknowledging these affects is not sufficient, especially given the negative influence some of them have on students' values and cultural beliefs. We also need to encourage the critical analysis of popular images, presenting students with art forms that challenge those images and offer alternative ways of constructing and reconstructing their own experience. Teachers can help students develop a critical understanding of the meaning and influence of such works. In the process, the students and their teacher may begin to redefine what schools are for, utilizing the power of the aesthetic for progressive purposes. Helping students develop a critical, analytical, reflective attitude toward those forms of popular culture in which they are immersed, but which are not always reflected upon, is central if we are to encourage not only the expression but the critical reexperiencing of those forms.

The difficulty of doing this in schools is intensified by the fact that forms of popular culture are usually seen as nonacademic or otherwise inappropriate within the curriculum. The ways in which we have separated elite from popular culture—both theoretically and practically—have generally resulted in a devaluation of art. If the arts are seen as created and appreciated only by a select few, or as the province of experts specially trained in the skills of criticism and appreciation, they lose an important part of their significance. In the process the arts become marginalized, unable to procure that sense of self- and other-realization, of individual sameness and difference, and of possibilities for improved forms of moral life and social interaction. We must not value the arts rhetorically while diminishing their actual range of influence.

In addition to exposing and critically assessing the messages conveyed through forms of popular culture, schools can take advantage of the creative potential of these forms to explore more positive images and directions. Again, we must keep in mind that an emphasis on certain values—equality, tolerance, respect for human life and the need for peace, and a commitment to some notion of a common good, for example—will not be significant for students unless they can come to understand the meanings of such ideals within their own aesthetically and socially reconstructed experience. If we are to facilitate some notion of an ethical culture in schools, one to which an altered form of aesthetic education might powerfully contribute, it is important that the personal, social, and political implications of moral values for our lives and actions, in and out of school, become a part of the overt curriculum. Hence it is crucial that we explore with students the vast potential that forms of popular culture have for changing individual experiences through altered forms of consciousness as well as for altering larger social realities.

I believe that the contextualization of the arts—their meaning for individual reconsiderations as well as social change—can be encouraged in schools through the analysis and production of student forms of popular culture. These productions have the capacity to connect what are often considered more distant moral imperatives and the real-life, flesh and blood experiences of young people in and out of school. The arts, as these capture both the meaning of common events and the possibilities for alternative experiences, understandings, and ways of life, might well make lasting contributions to this effort. In this way, the arts can do more than provide documentation of a group's ability to communicate and understand each other. They can, through the imaginative rendering of people, events, values, places, feelings, and ideas, help disclose worlds that are not yet in place and thus serve as a force to bring about their creation. This is the political promise of art, a promise to be fulfilled not through a narrow instrumentalism, but through its efficacy in helping us reflect on and transform our ways of life, our personal and social being, our sameness and difference.

Conclusions

The experiential patterns of our lives, and of our relationships with others, reveal both sameness and difference, making any simplistic linear theory of identity groundless. We recognize and value differences in ourselves over time, and within others at a given point in time, just as we see that such forms of variability help make us who we are. When we come to see things differently, to perceive both the natural and social worlds through different lenses, we pursue avenues for reexperiencing the conventional or the taken for granted. Through expanded experiences brought about by changes in our consciousness, we develop identities that are continuous with our previous selves. The arts, as symbolic creations capable of prodding our moral imaginations, enable us to re-envision personal and social experience and give us an important means of communicating and allowing for re-creation. Forms of popular culture, as conveyors of aesthetic experiences that are often carriers of ideological meaning, and that frequently create powerful experiences, need to be recognized for their personal and political influence and potential. The television programs, stories, movies, songs, etc., that young people experience should become part of the school curriculum and would help connect moral issues with personal experience. Recognizing the potential of popular culture for good or ill, teachers and students together might develop the forms of critical awareness that are necessary for pursuing personal and experiential revelation and social transformation. The development through schooling of an ethical culture in which popular art forms are analyzed as well as created provides one important route toward the role of schools in promoting social justice.

Notes

1. May Sarton, *Journal of a Solitude: The Intimate Diary of a Year in the Life of a Creative Woman* (New York: W. W. Norton & Company, 1973), p. 11.
2. Jerry Jeff Walker, "The Man He Used to Be," on his album *Hill Country Rain*, distributed by Rykodisc, Minneapolis, MN, 1992, recording number 7.
3. Landon E. Beyer and Daniel P. Liston, "Discourse or Moral Action? A Critique of Postmodernism," *Educational Theory* 42, no. 4 (Fall 1992): pp. 371–393.
4. See Landon E. Beyer, "Schooling for Democracy: What Kind?" in *The Curriculum: Problems, Politics, and Possibilities*, 2nd ed., Landon E. Beyer and Michael W. Apple, eds. (Albany: State University of New York Press, 1998), pp. 245–263.
5. See Maxine Greene, *Landscapes of Learning* (New York: Teachers College Press, 1978).
6. This is related to Paulo Freire's concept of "adaptation," as outlined in his *Education for Critical Consciousness* (New York: Seabury Press, 1973).
7. For this example, and for his feedback on the early version of this essay, I am indebted to Kenneth Teitelbaum.
8. Among other things, this poses problems for those in teacher education who seek to provide field experiences in the schools or elsewhere, experiences that are designed to foster certain altered attitudes or dispositions—for instance, an appreciation of cultural, ethnic, or other forms of diversity. See Landon E. Beyer, "Field Experience, Ideology, and the Development of Critical Reflectivity," *Journal of Teacher Education* 35, no. 3 (May-June 1984): pp. 36–41.
9. Ntozake Shange, *Betsey Brown: A Novel* (New York: St. Martin's Press, 1985).
10. For historic efforts to identify the essential elements of aesthetic experience, see chapters 1 and 2, above.
11. Judith Barry and Sandy Flitterman-Lewis, "Textual Strategies: The Politics of Art-Making," in *Feminist Art Criticism: An Anthology*, ed. Arlene Raven, Cassandra L. Langer, and Joanna Frueh (Ann Arbor: UMI Research Press, 1988), p. 88.
12. Raymond Williams, *The Long Revolution* (Harmondsworth, Middlesex, England: Chatto & Windus, 1961), pp. 64–65.
13. Maxine Greene, *Releasing the Imagination: Essays on Education, the Arts, and Social Change* (San Francisco: Jossey-Bass Publishers, 1995), pp. 4–5.

Epilogue: Creating New Worlds

Fortunately, there are many critical traditions, aesthetic resources, and progressive political movements on which educators can draw as we reconceive the arts and aesthetic education, in society and schools. Teachers can, working with their students, make plain the personal, material, and political value of aesthetic experiences. While the historical and contemporary resources that are available may not always be well known to teachers and the public at large, we need to acknowledge and draw upon the important legacies of art forms that can lead to critical, progressive, emancipatory possibilities.

In working toward cultural activities in schools that are nonreproductive, in creating and critically appreciating imaginative works of art that provide insight into present social conditions, in awakening the imaginative and visionary social possibilities that the arts provoke, in vivifying experiences that sometimes change who we are and what we think, and in seeing in these things that our identity may be enhanced, it seems to me that we act on the most important possibilities of articulating a democratic culture. Such a culture is clearly, in my view, in need of re-creation.

Cynicism abounds, and often for good reason. Many, though not all, contemporary college students find it hard to believe that people can and do purposefully act out of anything other than self-interest. The possibility that we might yet be able, together, to create a common good that speaks to ennobling human purposes and cultural values that encourage freedom while maintaining connections with others that are more than transitory seems, for many, to be out of reach. And the knowledge that social and economic inequalities in the United States and other industrialized nations continue to increase and the fact that forms of alienation appear more prevalent in many factories, offices, and families seem not to be taken as seriously as they once were. Such inequalities and forms of alienation continue at the same time that Wall Street creates new economic records almost daily. Yet this seems to go largely unnoticed, as do the interconnections of inequalities and forms of opulence. Is it really the case that Bill Gates needs, or deserves, a house worth, reportedly, nearly $50 million?

Many thoughtful, committed, creative teachers continue, against formidable odds, to provide engaging, personally moving, even transformative activities with their students. To note the fact that such activities are hardly the norm in most schools is not the point. Rather, we need to both acknowledge and learn from those teachers who have changed our and others' lives, even as they contribute to a more democratic classroom and way of life. How can we repay them?

Universities, too, are in need of help. Many are becoming more and more tightly connected to corporate agendas in terms of their internal structures, forms of language, and values and in their forms of allegiance. Technological initiatives continue to be underwritten by universities in the United States, to the benefit of what we continue to mistakenly call "private enterprise" undertakings. The socialization of costs and the privatization of benefits both manifest themselves through such state-corporate "partnerships" and are all too evident. Even what the university is for, or what its place is in the social order, becomes less and less clear, especially as the university and society become enmeshed in the "global economy." On the other hand, some colleges and universities have been able to maintain a kind of equilibrium that guides their identity over time, in part because they understand their roots, their commitments, and their history and in part because they have identified a set of values and ideals that outline what is, and is not, required of higher education institutions and programs.

The development of progressive art forms in the United States has a history, too, of course. I want to end this book by remembering and, more importantly, keeping alive aspects of that history and its connection to who and where we are, and perhaps where we are going.

In his study of Socialist Sunday schools that operated during the twentieth century, Kenneth Teitelbaum provides revealing and often inspiring examples of activities associated with these schools that provided clear alternatives to public-capitalist schools.[1] At one point, Teitelbaum discusses how one teacher, Helen Dunbar, attempted to create a series of activities on the topic of "water" as a way of indirectly teaching socialist ideas. A poem titled "Where Go the Boats," by Robert Louis Stevenson, was used with Ms. Dunbar's students:

Dark brown is the river,
Golden is the sand.
It flows along for ever,
With trees on either hand.
Green leaves afloating,
Castles in the foam,
Boats of mine aboating—
Where will all come home?
On goes the river
And out past the mill,
Away down the valley,
Away down the hill.
Away down the river,
A hundred miles or more.
Other little children
Shall bring my boats ashore.[2]

This short poem, utilized to reinforce the interrelatedness of people, provides one particular example of how the arts have conveyed to children messages that have helped shape their ways of thinking about and understanding their role in the larger society and the values that ought to underlie that role.

Eugene Debs was also moved by the arts, and in particular by certain literary works. His biographer writes that Daniel Debs, Eugene's father, lived in a house that, "contained two books that left an enduring mark on his oldest son. . . . [The most important] was *Les Misérables* [which] captured Debs' emotions. He read it time after time throughout his life, and each time he swore his allegiance to its central theme. He talked about it constantly. He recommended it equally to his friends and to casual acquaintances."[3] When Debs was jailed in 1919, he apparently was strengthened again by his reading of *Les Misérables*. His biographer reports that Debs "was perfectly reconciled to his situation. 'I'm here for a purpose,' he wrote to Horace Trambel, 'and I know how to be patient. The lessons I am learning here are of inestimable value to me, and I am not sorry that my lot is cast for a time among *Les Misérables*.' "[4]

Commitments to creating literary, musical, dramatic, cinematic, and other aesthetic forms to highlight and denounce various social injustices also have a long history in the United States. For example, in the foreword to *Carry It On! A History in Song and Picture of the Working Men and Women of America*, the authors warn the reader: "Beware! This is a book of history. With songs and pictures, we try to tell how the working people of this country—women and men; old and young;

people of various skin shades, various religions, languages, and national backgrounds—have tried to better their own lives and work toward a world of peace, freedom, jobs, and justice for all."[5] *Carry It On!* contains historical and contemporary songs, with words and musical notations included, that deal with issues related to the treatment of immigrants, women, factory workers, African Americans, and others, along with short narratives about the events portrayed in the songs. Among the songs included is "Harriet Tubman."

That particular song gained new meaning for me when I saw it performed in the moving tribute to working-class women who, in the 1920s and '30s, were enrolled in the Bryn Mawr Summer School for Working Women, as portrayed in the film *The Women of Summer.*[6] I first saw this film at an annual meeting of the American Educational Studies Association several years ago. I have watched it many times since then, with students and friends, and I see new things in it, and in me, whenever I view it. Each time its messages seem more moving, and more urgent.

The film celebrates the reunion of these women, who were for the most part former factory workers, and shows how the summer school changed their lives. One of the events chronicled in *The Women of Summer* is the trial and execution of Sacco and Vanzetti. For many of the Bryn Mawr enrollees, this and other struggles drew their attentions and energies and led to new forms of education, and eventually to new occupations and ways of life. A number of social causes were central to the lives of the students, many of whom went on to be union organizers, writers, and teachers.

I remember the first time that I viewed this film and the specific reactions that I had to the events surrounding the Sacco and Vanzetti trial. In addition to watching original film clips of the trial, I heard Hollie Near and Ronnie Gilbert perform a particularly powerful song by Charlie King, which deals with the events of the Sacco and Vanzetti trial:

"Two Good Arms"
Who will remember the hands so white and fine
That touched the finest linen, that poured the finest wine
Who will remember the genteel words they spoke
That named the lives of two good men a nuisance or a joke.

Chorus:
And all who know these two good arms
Know I never had to rob or kill
I can live by my own two hands and live well
And all my life I have struggled
To rid the earth of all such crimes.

Who will remember Judge Webster Thayer
One hand on the gavel, the other resting on the chair
Who will remember the hateful words he said
Speaking to the living in the language of the dead.

Chorus:
And all who know these two good arms
Know I never had to rob or kill
I can live by my own two hands and live well
And all my life I have struggled
To rid the earth of all such crimes.

Who will remember the hand that pulled the switch
That took the lives of two good men in the service of the rich
Who will remember the one who gave the nod
Or the chaplain standing near at hand to invoke the name of God.

Chorus:
And all who know these two good arms
Know I never had to rob or kill
I can live by my own two hands and live well
And all my life I have struggled
To rid the earth of all such crimes.

We will remember this good shoemaker
We will remember this poor fish peddler
We will remember all the strong arms and hands
That never once found justice in the hands that rule this land.

Chorus:
And all who knew these two good men
Knew they never had to rob or kill
Each had lived by his own two hands
And lived well
And all their lives they had struggled
To rid the earth of all such crimes.
And all our lives we must struggle
To rid the earth of all such crimes.[7]

Not long after I first heard the music and words to "Two Good Arms," I came to meet its author, Charlie King. I have in the intervening years come to know Charlie well. I admire his songs, his political commitments and determination, and his keen sense of humor. In many ways Charlie exemplifies those artists (musicians, poets, writers, actors, and others) who keep alive a vital tradition in American culture. The critical commentary, hopes, social analyses, and humor that they convey, and that continue to be portrayed in works of art that are aesthetically meaningful and politically insightful, provide us with hope and direction, and even inspiration. Working within this tradition, and in alliance with educators, community members, and students, we see ways to change the world. And that, finally, must be the point.

For many of my generation, and for me personally, one contemporary artist stands out as perhaps the most important poet and singer of that generation. Bob Dylan, through the music that he has written and performed for almost forty years, has perhaps had a greater impact on how we think about contemporary social issues than any other popular artist. His songs have seared and altered the consciousness of many, and they make clear how the arts contribute to understanding social life and contribute to social justice. A fitting end to this book is provided by a work by Bob Dylan that reminds us of the good that is yet to be done and its personal and social meaning:

"What Good Am I?"

What good am I
if I'm like all the rest,
If I just turn away
when I see how you're dressed,
If I shut myself off
so I can't hear ya cry,
What good am I?

What good am I
if I know and don't do,
If I see and don't say
if I look right through you,
If I turn a deaf ear
to the thunder in the sky,
What good am I?

What good am I
while you softly weep,
And I hear in my head
what ya say in your sleep,
An' I freeze in the moment
like the rest who don't try,
What good am I?

What good am I then
to others and me,
If I've had every chance
and yet still fail t' see,

If my hands are tied
 must I not wonder within,
Who tied them and why
 and where must I have been?

What good am I
 if I say foolish things,
And I laugh in the face of
 what sorrow brings,
An' I just turn my back
 while you silently die,
What good am I?[8]

Notes

1. Kenneth Teitelbaum, *Schooling for "Good Rebels": Socialism, American Education, and the Search for Radical Curriculum* (New York: Teachers College Press, 1995).

2. *Ibid.*, p. 148.

3. Ray Ginger, *The Bending Cross: A Biography of Eugene Victor Debs* (New York: Russell and Russell, 1949), p. 14.

4. Ibid., p. 388.

5. Pete Seeger and Bob Reiser, *Carry It On! A History in Song and Picture of the Working Men and Women of America* (New York: Simon and Schuster, 1985), p. 9.

6. *The Women of Summer*, produced by Suzanne Bauman, was funded through the National Endowment for the Humanities. It is available through Filmaker's Library, 133 East 58th Street, New York, NY 10022.

7. Charlie King, "Two Good Arms," copyright 1977, PIED ASP MUSIC (BMI). Charlie can be reached at: P.O. Box 6207, Hamden, CT 06517.

8. Bob Dylan, "What Good Am I?" on *Oh Mercy*, Columbia Records, New York, 1989, recording number 7.

Index

achievement model, 51
Aeschylus, 37
aesthetic, defined, 4
aesthetic attitude theories, 26–34
aesthetic experience, 1–20, 44, 68, 90
  defined, 1
  and social realities, 67–67, 80–81
aesthetic forms, 69–70
aesthetic meaning, 68–73
aesthetic perception, 6, 9–10, 28–30
aesthetic response, as dialectic, 38
aesthetic theory, 70, 83–85, 90–91, 100–5
  defined, 1, 4
aesthetic value, 7, 82, 90
aesthetics
  and ideology, 72
  and materialism,91–100
Apple, Michael W., 56
Arnstine, Donald, 39, 40, 41
art
  defined, 1, 2
  instruction, 109–24
  perceptual qualities, 10–15
  and physical distance, 7–15
  political and social implications, 85
  presentational, 34
  and psychological distance, 7
  and social life, 89–91
art for art's sake movement, 10
artifactual, defined, 1
artistic mediums, 2
art object, 1, 3, 7
arts, the
  in American life, 2
  attitudinal approaches, 3–7
  budget cuts, 2
  communication, 103–4
  elitist nature, 12
  fine vs. popular, 103
  socially constructed nature, 82–84, 104–5
  support of, 2

Balzac, Honoré de, 76
Barrett, Michele, 78–79
Barry, Judith, 80, 81–82
Baumgarten, Alexander Gottleib, 4
Beardsley, Monroe, 14, 15
Beauty, 9–10
Bell, Clive, 11
Berger, John
  Ways of Seeing, 74–77
Berlak, Ann, 115
Berlak, Jarold, 115
Bernstein, Basil, 57–59
bourgeoisie, 91–92
Bowles, Samuel, and Gintis, Herbert
  Schooling in Capitalist America, 52–54, 55
Bredo, Eric, 17
Broudy, Harry, 11
Bryn Mawr Summer School for Working Women, 150
Bullough, Edward, 7–9
  "Psychical Distance. . .," 7

Burchfield, Charles
Black Houses, 39, 40

capitalism, 18
Carnegie Commission, 100
de Castell, Suzanne, 67–68, 80–81
censorship, 92–93
Central Midwestern Regional Education Laboratory (CEMREL), 42–43, 49
Chapman, Laura, 12, 102
Chicago, Judy, 81
The Dinner Party, 79
Church fathers, 4
commodification, 18–20
content, 32
Coppola, Francis Ford,
Apocalypse Now, 31, 90
Coward, Rosalind, 78–79
Crittenden, Brian, 115
cultural elite, 12, 101–2, 143
cultural politics, 81–84
curriculum, 49–52, 58, 109–11, 120–21

Debs, Eugene, 149
Dewey, John, 115
disinterestedness, 5–9
Dreeben, Robert
"On What Is Learned in School," 50–51
Dunbar, Helen, 148–49
Dylan, Bob, 35
"Hurricane," 35, 36
"Wat Good Am I?" 152–53

Eagleton, Terry, 61
economics, 71
and schooling, 52–55
education
aesthetic, 83, 100–5, 140–44
as cultural reproduction, 55–61
as economic reproduction, 52–55
reproduction in, 49–52
Edwards, Richard, 16, 54
Engels, Friedrich, 91, 93–100
The Holy Family, 95

Feinberg, Walter, 17
feminist aesthetics, 77–82
feminist criticism, 80
Flitterman-Lewis, Sandy, 80–82
"fine arts" v. "popular arts," 15
Floud, J., 52, 64
form, 40
Formalist approach, 27–28, 85, 90

Gates, Bill, 148
Gilbert, Ronnie, 150–1
Goethe, J.W. von, 93
Goodman, Nelson, 36–37
Gramsci, Antonio, 59
Greek philosophers, 4
Greene, Maxine, 141–2

Hals, Frans, 74–76
Regentesses of The Old Men's Alms House, 74–76
Regents of The Old Men's Alms House, 74–76
Halsey, A.H., 52
Hugo, Victor
Les Misérables, 149
Huyssen, Andreas, 79
"Mass Culture as Woman," 79

ideology, 72
Ingarden, Roman, 9
instrumental rationality, 15–18
interest, defined, 5

Kant, Immanuel, 4
The Critique of Judgment, 4–5
King, Charlie
"Two Good Arms," 150–1
Kliebard, Herbert M., 52

Lasch, Christopher, 16–17, 19
Lassalle, Ferdinand
Franz von Sickengen, 93, 94, 98
Lifshitz, Mikhail, 97
literature, as commodity, 92–93
logic, 17

Marx, Karl, 71–72, 78, 91–100
aesthetic theory, 98–100
The German Ideology, 60–61

The Holy Family, 95
mass production, 18–20
meaning, 35, 41
defined, 26–27
Milton, John, 92

National Commission on Excellence in Education
A Nation at Risk, 101
Near, Hollie, 150

Parker, DeWitt, 27
Pepper, Stephen, 27
performing arts, 101
phenomenological objectivity, 43
Picasso, Pablo, 19
Guernica, 19, 28–29
Plato, vii, 1
positivism, 17–1
postmodernism, 80
"Presentational Aesthetic, " 25–26
press, freedom of the , 92
private property, 58
psychical distance, 7–15

racism, 84
"radical pluralism," 68
Reiser, Bob
Carry It On!, 149–150
Robinson, Lillian S.
Sex, Class, and Culture, 78

Sacco and Vanzetti trial, 150–1
Sarton, May, 129
Seeger, Pete
Carry It On!, 149–150
Shaftesbury, Lord, 5
Showalter, Elaine, 80
significance, 30
defined, 26–28
social commitment, and aesthetic value, 116–19
social communication
the arts as, 137–40
commonality and difference, 131–32
experience and expression, 133–37
social context, 35–38
Socialist Realism, 99
socialization, 51–53
Springsteen, Bruce, 117
Stevenson, Robert Louis, 148–49
Stolnitz, Jerome, 5, 9
"structure of feeling," 69–70
Sue, Eugene
The Mysteries of Paris, 95–98
Szeliga, FIRST NAME?????? 95–97

teacher preparation
and aesthetic meanings, 119–24
and critical inquiry, 111–16
technicism, 15–19
Teitelbaum, Kenneth, 148
television, 72–74
"things known" 4
"things perceived,"4

Vivas, Eliseo, 13

Walker, Jerry Jeff
"The Man He Used to Be," 129–31
Williams, Raymond, 68–74, 76, 102–3, 139
The Long Revolution, 68–69
Willis, Paul, 59
women, treatment of, 84
Women of Summer, The, 150
women's experience, 138
Woolf, Virginia, 79
A Room of One's Own, 77
Wright, Eric Olin, 48

Young, Michael F.D., 55–56
Young German Movement, 98

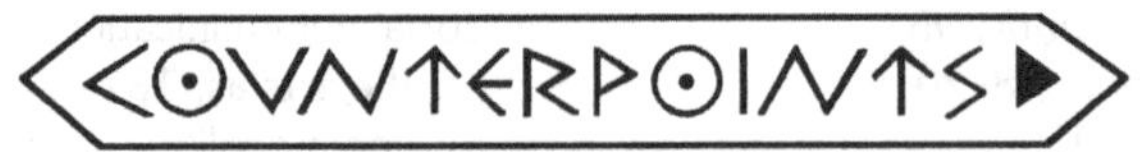

Studies in the Postmodern Theory of Education

General Editor
Shirley R. Steinberg

Counterpoints publishes the most compelling and imaginative books being written in education today. Grounded on the theoretical advances in criticalism, feminism, and postmodernism in the last two decades of the twentieth century, Counterpoints engages the meaning of these innovations in various forms of educational expression. Committed to the proposition that theoretical literature should be accessible to a variety of audiences, the series insists that its authors avoid esoteric and jargonistic languages that transform educational scholarship into an elite discourse for the initiated. Scholarly work matters only to the degree it affects consciousness and practice at multiple sites. Counterpoints' editorial policy is based on these principles and the ability of scholars to break new ground, to open new conversations, to go where educators have never gone before.

For additional information about this series or for the submission of manuscripts, please contact:

Shirley R. Steinberg
c/o Peter Lang Publishing, Inc.
29 Broadway, 18th floor
New York, New York 10006

To order other books in this series, please contact our Customer Service Department:

(800) 770-LANG (within the U.S.)
(212) 647-7706 (outside the U.S.)
(212) 647-7707 FAX

Or browse online by series:

www.peterlang.com

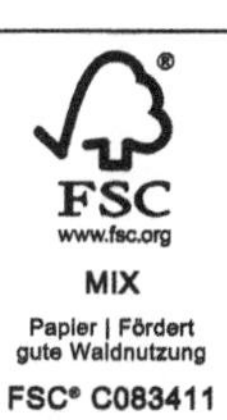

Zeitfracht Medien GmbH
Ferdinand-Jühlke-Straße 7
99095 Erfurt, Deutschland
produktsicherheit@kolibri360.de